backblocks
america

backblocks america

JO AND GARETH MORGAN
TAKE ON THE STATES CANADA AND MEXICO

RANDOM HOUSE
NEW ZEALAND

Morgan, Gareth (Gareth H. T.)
Backblocks America : Jo and Gareth Morgan take on the States,
Mexico and Canada / Gareth Morgan, Jo Morgan.
ISBN 978-1-86941-888-5
1. United States—Description and travel. 2. Canada—Description
and travel. 3. Mexico—Description and travel. I. Morgan, Jo.
II. Title.
917.04—dc 22

A RANDOM HOUSE BOOK
published by
Random House New Zealand
18 Poland Road, Glenfield, Auckland, New Zealand
www.randomhouse.co.nz

Random House International
Random House
20 Vauxhall Bridge Road
London, SW1V 2SA
United Kingdom

Random House Australia (Pty) Ltd
20 Alfred Street, Milsons Point, Sydney,
New South Wales 2061, Australia

Random House South Africa Pty Ltd
Isle of Houghton
Corner Boundary Road and Carse O'Gowrie
Houghton 2198, South Africa

Random House Publishers India Private Ltd
301 World Trade Tower, Hotel Intercontinental Grand Complex,
Barakhamba Lane, New Delhi 110 001, India

First published 2007
© 2007 Gareth and Jo Morgan

Text design: Sharon Grace
Cover design: Katy Yiakmis
Author photograph: Chris Coad
Maps: Holly Roach
Printed in Australia by Griffin Press

CONTENTS

MAP KEY

1. Eleuthera Island, Bahamas
2. Miami, Florida
3. St Augustine, Florida
4. Charleston, South Carolina
5. Jamestown, Williamsburg, Virginia
6. Warrenton, Virginia
7. Ligonier, Pennsylvania
8. Parkman, Ohio
9. Morgantown, West Virginia
10. Harrisonburg, Virginia
11. Roanoke, Virginia
12. Townsend, Tennessee
13. Stecoah, North Carolina
14. Atlanta, Georgia
15. Chattanooga, Tennessee
16. Nashville, Tennessee
17. Memphis, Tennessee
18. Birmingham, Alabama
19. Selma, Alabama
20. Vicksburg, Mississippi
21. Natchez, Mississippi
22. Baton Rouge, Louisiana
23. New Orleans, Louisiana
24. Gibson, Louisiana
25. San Antonio, Texas
26. Laredo, Texas
27. Monclova, Mexico
28. Torreon, Mexico
29. Balleza, Mexico
30. Batopilas, Mexico
31. Creel, Mexico
32. Chihuahua, Mexico
33. Terlingua, Texas
34. Pecos, Texas
35. Alamogordo, New Mexico
36. Santa Fe, New Mexico
37. Cortez, Colorado
38. Grand Canyon, Arizona
39. Page, Arizona
40. Pleasant Creek, Utah
41. Moab, Utah
42. Yellowstone, Wyoming
43. Billings, Montana
44. Kalispell, Montana

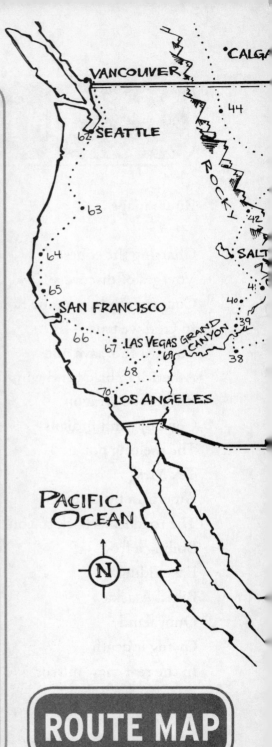

ROUTE MAP

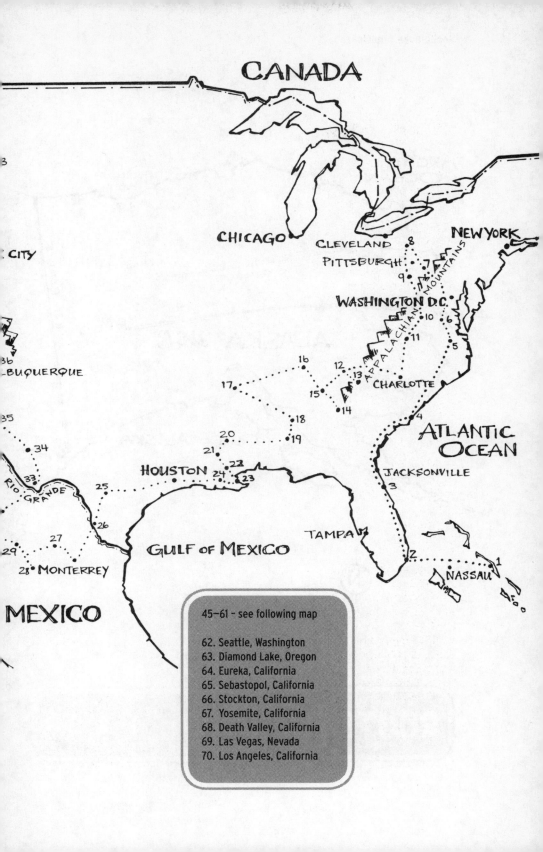

CANADA

CHICAGO
CLEVELAND
PITTSBURGH
: CITY
3
WASHINGTON D.C.
NEW YORK
8
7
9
10 6
11
5
16
17   12
13 CHARLOTTE
15 14
18
19
20
21
24 22
23
HOUSTON
25
26
27
29
28 MONTERREY
RIO GRANDE
33
34
35
36
BUQUERQUE
MOUNTAINS
APPALACHIAN
ATLANTIC
OCEAN
JACKSONVILLE
4
3
TAMPA
2
1
NASSAU
GULF OF MEXICO
MEXICO

45–61 - see following map

62. Seattle, Washington
63. Diamond Lake, Oregon
64. Eureka, California
65. Sebastopol, California
66. Stockton, California
67. Yosemite, California
68. Death Valley, California
69. Las Vegas, Nevada
70. Los Angeles, California

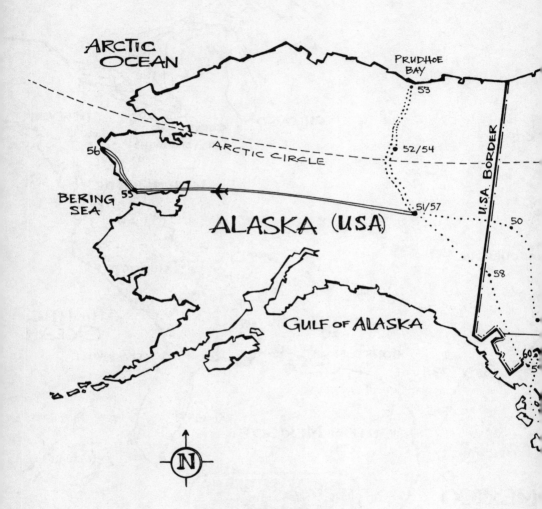

ARCTIC
OCEAN

PRUDHOE
BAY
• 53

ARCTIC CIRCLE

• 52/54

U.S.A. BORDER

56

BERING 55
SEA

ALASKA (USA)

• 51/57

50

• 58

GULF of ALASKA

60

N

PACIFIC
OCEAN

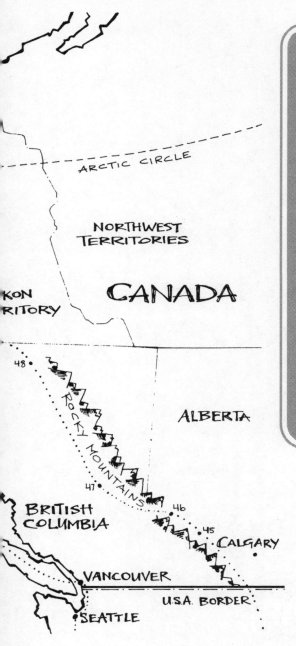

ARCTIC CIRCLE

NORTHWEST
TERRITORIES

KON
RITORY

CANADA

48

ROCKY MOUNTAINS

ALBERTA

47

46

BRITISH
COLUMBIA

45

CALGARY

VANCOUVER

U.S.A. BORDER

SEATTLE

MAP KEY

45. Radium Hot Springs, British Columbia
46. Jasper, Alberta
47. Prince George, British Columbia
48. Moose Meadow, British Columbia
49. Whitehorse, Yukon
50. Dawson City, Yukon
51. Fairbanks, Alaska
52. Coldfoot, Alaska
53. Deadhorse, Alaska
54. Coldfoot, Alaska
55. Nome, Alaska (by air from Fairbanks)
56. Bering Land Bridge National Park
57. Fairbanks, Alaska
58. Beaver Creek, Yukon
59. Haines, Alaska
60. Inner Passage Highway (Skagway to Port Hardy on Vancouver Island)
61. Vancouver, British Columbia

CHARTING THE COURSE

I t was probably in Kyrgyzstan that the idea came to us. We were slightly more than halfway through our epic 2004 traverse of the Silk Road route from Venice to Beijing in the footsteps of the great Venetian traveller Marco Polo. We were full of the joys of adventure motorcycling and — if it was indeed Kyrgyzstan — probably a mug of fermented mare's milk too. The only cloud on our spiritual horizon was the depressing knowledge that this trip of trips would soon end and that it was likely to be not only the pinnacle of our motorcycling careers but also a highlight of our lives. What could we possibly do next that would compare?

Before the Silk Road we'd ridden extensively in New Zealand and had made trips to the Indian Himalaya, to Nepal and to the Andes region of South America. Our preparation for the Silk Road had entailed a shakedown trip to the Australian outback. By the end of the Silk Road we'd left the tracks of our knobbly tyres across a decent portion of the world.

So why not keep going, we wondered. Why not carry on and do the world by bike?

And that's how the World By Bike concept was born.

Gareth got straight onto one of the guys in the office back in Wellington, New Zealand, and asked him to draw lines on a world map connecting the trips we'd already done. When the result arrived by return email a day or so later, Gareth showed it to our old biking mate and fellow Silk Rider Dave Wallace.

'There,' he said triumphantly. 'That's what Jo and I are going to do.'

Dave's face, lit by the monitor, was a picture of wistfulness.

'Of course,' Gareth continued. 'You probably won't have the time or finances to come along.'

Dave shrugged. 'How the hell will the pair of you pull something like that off without me along to look after you? I'll have to bloody do it, won't I?'

That sounded like a 'yes' — just the response we'd been hoping for.

It wasn't until later on, when we studied the map in more detail, that we realised there was a downside. Doing the world by bike committed us to going to America.

Bugger, we thought. Who wanted to do that?

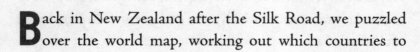

Back in New Zealand after the Silk Road, we puzzled over the world map, working out which countries to do in which order, bearing in mind the seasonal constraints on visiting many of them. We had no immediate plans to visit North America, although we were resigned to doing it sooner or later. But around this time we learned that another biking buddy of ours, Mike O'Donnell (MoD), was planning a motorbike trip to the States in mid-2006. His wife Alex — alias 'the Redhead' — was from Montana and they were heading back to visit her family. They were also keen to catch a music festival in Austin, Texas, and MoD thought it would be cool to combine both into a biking trip from Texas up the Rocky Mountains into Canada, Alaska and the Pacific Northwest of America.

Mike is business manager of the TradeMe auction website founded by our son Sam. He would have been a certain starter on the Silk Road if only he'd had the time. We've done a fair bit of riding with MoD; he's a great rider and always stimulating — read 'unpredictable' — company. His trademarks are the single malts and Havanas with which everyone rounds off a day's riding when he's around. Well, all that was before MoD had his young family and entered a new phase of life in which he has had to sacrifice some of his outings with his reprobate mates. We all understand and remember those days.

But while we were happy joining MoD on tour, his itinerary sounded a little bit too scenic for Gareth. For while MoD's interests lay in the top left-hand corner of the continent, Gareth's were strictly in the bottom right: the Old South of the Civil War, slavery and the civil rights movement, not to mention the music — blues, jazz, bluegrass and the roots of rock'n'roll.

Still, whereas MoD could only spare three weeks on the road, four at the most, we were footloose and fancy-free now the kids had flown the nest and we could stretch things out a little longer. Why not weld the two itineraries together? After all, MoD didn't have to be along for the whole ride.

As he began to research the possibilities of this approach, Gareth's mouth started watering. There were places he wanted to visit after all.

But what he really needed was a reason to go — a theme or a purpose to give the trip meaning within the World By Bike framework.

The logical place to start a trip to America, he figured, would be the point at which Christopher Columbus first sighted the New World. In researching Columbus, Gareth discovered that the first landfall wasn't in America at all, it was in the Bahamas. Well, adding a Caribbean holiday would be a hardship! And then he made another discovery. Columbus owned and extensively annotated a copy of *Il Milione*, the story of Marco Polo's trip to the Far East, and one of his motives in setting out on the voyage that landed him in America was to pioneer a sea route to the East Indies of which Polo spoke.

That was our link, right there, Gareth decided. That was the justification for going to America next and the excuse we needed for going at all.

As the itinerary came together on one of Gareth's beloved spreadsheets, other links fortuitously showed up. Someone drew our attention to retired Royal Navy submariner and amateur historian Gavin Menzies's *1421: The Year China Discovered the World*, which argues quite persuasively that a fleet of Chinese junks made landfall in America decades before Columbus. Our Silk Road adventure finished up in China — and now we discovered that America belonged to the Chinese!

When he learned of our plans to go to the United States, Gareth's brother, Tim, presented him with a well-thumbed copy of *Bury My Heart at Wounded Knee* by Dee Brown, which tells the real story of the relationship between the European cowboys and the American Indians that we've all grown up with — you know, the whole 'Here come the redskins. Get those wagons in a circle, pilgrim' thing.

Gareth read it and was transfixed. Man, this trip had it all: exotic landscapes, music, history — and now ethnic cleansing and genocide.

That, of course, got him started on the origins of the American Indians, who are thought to have entered North America during the last ice age via a land bridge that then linked Siberia and Alaska. The logical place to start was there, at the western extremity of the American land mass, but there was MoD's timetable to accommodate and the limited season in which Alaska is accessible to consider. It would have to be enough to include the point of first human contact with America somewhere in the itinerary, albeit out of order.

Meanwhile, Jo remained unconvinced about the whole venture. While neither of us has anything against the genteel motorcycle touring you do on good roads, eating good food, overnighting in quality accommodation, never straying too far from medical and mechanical assistance — and we've done a few cappuccino canters in our time — it's adventure motorbiking that really spins our wheels. The frustrations, the fear, the loathing you experience travelling through countries where you don't know the language; the punctures, the potholes, the traffic hazards, the ups and downs — they're what make the whole enterprise memorable. You need a bit of adversity because, as our resident economist will tell you, without risk there's no reward. Of the two of us, Jo feels more strongly about this point. She's firmly into exotica. She enjoys the challenge of negotiating language barriers — it engages her grey matter in a way that meeting and greeting in English doesn't. Predominantly white, Anglo-Saxon, Protestant and English-speaking (in a fashion) America just didn't do it for her.

So whereas Gareth had drawn up an itinerary that took us as far south as New Orleans and then meandered up to Santa Fe, she wondered why we weren't dipping south across the border into Mexico. At least it would be a bit of relief from the monoculture.

Done! We were off to Mexico.

But we weren't finished yet. Gareth was still chafing at the unrelentingly genteel roads and sizeable towns we would be traversing on MoD's section of the journey. What, he asked himself and MoD, was the point? The Alaskan leg looked to him like an opportunity lost. MoD had us finishing up in Fairbanks, whereas it appeared to Gareth that there were roads leading further north — far further north. Why not try to get as far north as you could thrash a bike? Say, to the Arctic Ocean? That would give us something to do.

One of MoD's strengths is the preparation he puts into his trips. His forward research of the roads he intends taking borders on the obsessive. He certainly rose to the Alaskan challenge and before long we were lining up the road that services the Prudhoe Bay oil pipeline, one of American motorcycling's epic routes.

And of course, once he was on board, bloody Dave had to stick his oar in too. Like Jo, Dave was lukewarm on America. So far as he was concerned, the United States was an old man's motorbiking destination, devoid of challenges. Still, if we were going, we were going, and we'd have to make the most of it. If we really had to go to America, the bit that Dave most wanted to do was to ride down the Pacific coast to California. MoD had his trip finishing in Seattle and Gareth had been happy to go along with that. But Dave made a strong case.

No problem Dave, we said. We'll just add another few thousand kilometres to the trip. So long as everyone's happy!

Everyone *was* happy. By the time we'd hammered it all out we couldn't wait to start.

The next question was who goes?

We had put the idea to Dave Wallace but as he would be in the throes of building his new house over the months concerned he had to think about it.

Five seconds later he said: 'Yep. Count me in.'

We've known him and ridden with him for years. Dave's an automatic selection on an expedition ride. He's a gem, even if he is a gem in the rough. He can be direct to the point of abrasiveness and he can be crude, crass and insensitive

— not like Gareth, of course. But so what? Against that, he's the perfect team player, always looking out for the rest of us. No one gets left behind if Dave has anything to do with it. He's a strong, capable rider, a practical and knowledgeable bush mechanic and a reassuring physical presence in any threatening situation.

Besides Dave, none of the rest of the crew from the Silk Road — Phil Lough, Bryan Wyness, Brendan Keogh or Selwyn Blinkhorne — could spare the time for this one. We could have left it at the four of us — Gareth, Jo, Dave and MoD — but as MoD was only joining us for some of the second half of the trip, Dave would be obliged to pay for single accommodation when we weren't tenting.

'Or we could share with him,' Gareth suggested.

'No way,' replied Jo, with a randy gleam in her eye.

So all things considered it made sense to try to find another rider.

The Silk Road adventure generated an enormous amount of interest and even before our return from that trip we were inundated with correspondence from bikers keen to join our next excursion. Occasionally Gareth would get pissed off with a peremptory letter or email that would read like a booking, as though we were running an adventure holiday service. These got short shrift. Some of the others were more credible and compelling. Our standard tactic in response was to turn the heat back on the person making the approach, asking them to justify their selection. Why, we asked them, would we want them along? Why would we bother? And we'd also point out the demands of the trip; not only the duration — four months is a long time for anyone to be doing nothing but having fun in the modern world — but also the expense. If you didn't have $30K to toss down the hole it just wasn't worth considering coming along. It probably wouldn't cost that much but if things turned to custard everyone had to be able to get themselves out of it, whatever the price. The realities, once pointed out, deflected the bulk of the wannabes.

One of those who wrote to enquire whether there would be a place on the American trip was a Manawatu farmer named Roger Clausen. When challenged to produce his credentials, he wrote that he'd already ridden across America once on an organised tour of Harley-Davidson riders. This and the fact that as a farmer he was likely to be quite practical were in his favour. We added him to the long list of possibles.

Some time later we were in Palmerston North doing a charity gig, one of a series of presentations we did around the regions about the Silk Road trip. As we had no real notion of which local charities were the most deserving in each region, we asked the committee organising each event to decide which charity should benefit. Just before the Palmerston North gig, Gareth was approached by the chairman of the committee, who turned out to be Roger. He asked whether he could do an introduction to Gareth's presentation and Gareth readily assented. As Roger spoke, relaxed, confident, charming and witty, Gareth decided this fellow had personality. He might be a starter.

Not that it was solely his — or even our — decision. It would be Dave who'd have to share a room with the bloke. Gareth phoned Dave and told him about Roger. Dave came down to Palmerston North from Tauranga and, with Gareth, interviewed Roger for the final spot. Dave is pretty hard to please but he professed himself happy. Soon afterwards Roger and his wife Marian came down to Wellington to help us with the selection of equipment with the trip. We all got on fine. Roger was in.

Before the Silk Road trip we staged an epic and extremely valuable shakedown expedition to the Australian outback. There was less need this time — in America we wouldn't be facing the technical difficulties we had in the underdeveloped countries of Central Asia.

We did, however, have one ride as a group from Wellington up to Paraparaumu, a mere 50 km on good roads. It was a short ride but even so a potential problem emerged almost immediately. Roger was used to riding the way they do in those Harley-Davidson convoys, where everyone is up the bum of the rider in front. It's not how we prefer to do things. We insist on a bit of space to allow for the sudden braking or steering manoeuvres you tend to do in rugged country, either because something forces you to — a dog jumping out at you or a pothole looming — or because you see something you want to stop or turn off for.

Even Harley convoys have their moments with the tailgating formation they adopt. We learned that our mate Bryan Wyness — Captain Bryan of Silk Riders fame — had been along on the Harley tour of the States that Roger had mentioned. Bryan had been so concerned about how closely he was being followed by another Kiwi rider that he'd had words to him about it. The very next day, and in spite of this warning, when Bryan was forced to make a sudden turn, he'd been T-boned by his tailgating compatriot. Both he and his wife Marion, who was riding pillion, had been spilled onto the road and, while not seriously injured, they were badly shaken and very seriously pissed off.

To prevent such an event on the United States tour, Gareth distributed the same sheet outlining rider etiquette that he'd drawn up for the Silk Road, with a minor amendment for Roger's benefit.

'Only dickheads ride too close,' it read.

There were a few teething problems — as there always are with our system since it's not everyone's natural game — but they were minor. Once we were on tour Roger got the hang of it nicely. He was probably on dicier ground when, after a long day quite early on in the trip, he made the mistake of putting his arm round Jo's shoulders and telling her how well she'd done. Gareth and Dave winced and stood back to see what would happen. To their astonishment, nothing much did. But a couple of days later, after an equally gruelling day, Jo slung an arm round Roger's shoulders and told him he'd done really well 'for an old fella'.

Her point was taken. It became something of a standing joke between them for the rest of the tour.

VOYAGES
OF DISCOVERY

Christopher Columbus departed from Palos in Spain on 3 August 1492, boldly striking out across the Ocean Sea (as the Atlantic was then known) in search of a western route to China and the East Indies, against the advice of his countrymen and the better judgment of his crew.

In the wee hours of 12 October, as if to vindicate his faith in the new-fangled notion that the world was round like a ball not flat like a coin, one of his crew sighted waves crashing on the shore of the Americas.

You beauty, Columbus said. China.

Of course it wasn't China — or even India — that Columbus had discovered, but nor was it America. Or at least not yet. Columbus didn't suspect the American mainland existed, let alone set foot on it, until his third voyage six years later. His first landfall was actually somewhere in the

Bahamas, one of the chains of islands that dot the Caribbean Sea to the east of Central America.

Contrary to popular belief, no one involved with Columbus' enterprise really thought the world was flat. But Columbus did subscribe to the view that the earth was six parts land to one part sea, so when he read Marco Polo's account of the Far East he concluded that Polo was far further east when he reached Xanadu than the famous Venetian believed he was. Columbus was confident that there was nothing but briny between the Canary Islands and the coast of China — or at least the seven thousand islands that Marco Polo claimed lay just to the east of Cathay.

There was a fair bit of disagreement about just how much briny there was. Before Columbus managed to persuade the jointly ruling monarchs of two of Spain's largest kingdoms to invest in his trans-Atlantic venture, he hawked the prospectus around the maritime powers of Europe. In the course of doing due diligence, both the Portuguese and the English were advised by their experts that Columbus's estimate of the distance he'd have to sail — he reckoned just 2400 nautical miles — was wildly optimistic. Even King Ferdinand and Queen Isabella, his eventual backers, received similar advice and probably had no high expectation of seeing him — or their money — ever again.

His lousy maths, and a bit of confusion over whether the calculations should be done in Arabic or Italian miles, led Columbus to believe there was a shore 2400 miles west of the coast of Europe. In fact the distance around the globe from the Canaries to China is 10,600 nautical miles, well outside the range of ocean-going European ships in those days. But, according to rumours that were rife before he set sail, he had come by a chart of a coast just 2400 miles west, made by someone who had already been there. This proved correct and would account for his otherwise suicidal certainty.

If he'd had a mind to, Columbus could have put together an expedition to cross the Atlantic by himself, hiring a ship and a crew on his own account. Instead he sought official patronage. It was important to him that he could claim any new lands he discovered under the name of a European power — how else could he stake a claim to a share in the spoils of exploitation? The English and the Portuguese were interested in his proposal but ultimately didn't believe he could accomplish it. For all their own doubts, the Spanish Catholic monarchs Ferdinand and Isabella — mostly Isabella — were prepared to take a punt and they arranged for three vessels to be commandeered from their private owners for Columbus. They were a pair of caravels, the *Niña* and the *Pinta*, and a larger vessel to carry supplies, the *Santa Maria*.

Regardless of whether Columbus knew of the existence of America, it is unquestionably true that he was not the first to discover it. The 'Indians' — the indigenous inhabitants of the Americas — got there first. And by the time Columbus set sail the Vikings had been singing for decades about a country named Vinland, discovered by nautical Norseman Leif Ericson roughly where America should be; concrete evidence of their encounter with the New World has duly turned up in the shape of the remains of a Viking village in Newfoundland. There are countless, tantalising hints in the traditions and literatures of other cultures too and theories have been advanced down the years to suggest any number of explorers and all sorts of nations had discovered America long before our man Columbus — everyone from an African emperor named Abubakari II, an Irish monk named Brendan and the ancestors of the Polynesians, to the Japanese, the Chinese, the followers of the unlikely sounding cult of Jared, one of the lost tribes of Israel, the Welsh and, of course, aliens.

All founding myths are contestable. Much of what most Americans — and the Spanish and Portuguese — believe and celebrate about the discovery of America is inaccurate. Columbus wasn't the first. He wasn't even Spanish or Portuguese by birth, he was from Genoa in Italy. And his name wasn't really Columbus either. That's a Latinised version of his real name, Cristobal Colon. The popular record has it that Columbus was named after a dove rather than, as it seems, after a large intestine.

On the Silk Road we rode bikes that were supplied at a price that fairly reflected our 'value-add' for BMW. It proved to be a mutually advantageous arrangement. The 650cc Dakars were up there as one of the preferred machines for our purposes and in return the Silk Riders provided BMW with the kind of product-testing programme and publicity that money just can't buy.

While we were aiming to steer clear of the Interstate highways, the roads in the United States were still likely to be far better than we had experienced in less developed parts of the world. Without as much off-road or rough road work there was less chance of 'dropping' the bikes. We could therefore afford the luxury of heavier machines and more horsepower. The notion of doing America by Harley had a certain appeal, but we didn't want to disqualify ourselves from hitting the rough stuff when the chance came our way, as it would in Mexico's Copper Canyon and north of Fairbanks in Alaska. The memory of a Harley Road King self-dismantling on our tour of the Australian outback was ingrained in our minds so *Easy Rider* romance made way for practicality.

We were also already thinking ahead to the African leg of the World By Bike enterprise and we were keen to try out the larger BMW off-roaders to see how they compared with the 650s. Dave already owned a couple of them so needed little persuasion. Dave, Roger and Gareth therefore chose BMW R1200 GS bikes, though Jo (aka 'Stumpy') opted to stick with the F650 GS — a machine on lower suspension that didn't present her with the precarious problem of having to keep the bike upright on tiptoes when astride it at a standstill. MoD had chosen to bring his KTM 950 Adventure along and we graciously allowed it — provided he stayed out of the official photographs.

BMW offered us a similar deal on this trip to the previous adventure, confirming that the Silk Road partnership had worked for them. Sponsorship deals for adventure bike rides are not a no-brainer for the manufacturer. Month after month of riding in tough conditions really does test the machines and, when there's a fair glare of publicity involved, their product is in the spotlight for better or for worse. The bikes hadn't survived the Silk Road journey entirely unscathed so the fact BMW were up for it again is testimony to their own adventurous ethos and, ultimately, their confidence that the machines would meet the challenges we'd throw at them. From our perspective, we'd concluded that these bikes were a good option for the long, hard adventure ride ahead so the company's decision to partner us in the enterprise was of mutual benefit.

Other sponsors from the Silk Road adventure stepped back into the fray as well, which pleased us, as again we were choosing to use their products for the simple reason that they were the best for the job. So Icebreaker clothing kept the crew warm in the Arctic and cool in Death Valley while John Baker Insurance mustered sufficient courage to insure us. At least they didn't face the challenge of arranging cover in such tough destinations as Iran and Uzbekistan this time around.

Fairydown had a tougher row to hoe. We'd made some pretty heavy demands on their tents on the Silk Road but this time round we really wanted them to be bear-proof, a quality that hadn't exactly been uppermost in their minds when they briefed their designers. After one night lying snug in our tents while a bear ripped the soft-top off a Mustang convertible parked a hundred metres away, it has to be said we wondered about the wisdom of tenting at all.

With all our riding gear stuffed into crates with the bikes and consigned to America from Tauranga, three of us — Gareth, Jo and Dave — departed New Zealand on 12 April 2006. First touchdown on United States soil was at LAX, where we were subjected to the full rigour of a Customs check in the post-9/11 Home of the Brave. We'd taken the precaution of padlocking our luggage but the locks were snipped off and our bags thoroughly searched by the defenders of the Land of the Free, who left notices in the bags explaining the Homeland Security policy of randomly selecting luggage for this type of treatment. A meticulous ransacking notwithstanding, we were ushered through the border formalities at a speed that should make Customs and Immigration in New Zealand airports hang their heads in shame. The officials were cool but courteous at all times — the latter attribute typical of Americans, as we were to discover.

To preserve the element of freedom and spontaneity, we have a policy of making as few advance travel and accommodation arrangements as possible on our trips.

While he was in the wireless hotspot at the airport, it occurred to Gareth that this might be a good time to look into travel for the Bahamas leg of the trip. He managed to get us five-day return tickets out of Miami, Florida, to Nassau, the gateway to the Bahamas. That was sorted. We relaxed.

Freedom and spontaneity are all very well, but once we were on the ground at Nassau it looked for a moment as though we were going to come unstuck, as it was Easter weekend. We sweltered in the sticky Caribbean heat amid the confusion at the airport, a pretty basic affair consisting of a tarmac airstrip and a large tin shed for a terminal — not unlike the facilities at Apia in Samoa — trying to work out our onward travel plans. The prospects were not bright. At Easter the Bahamas are overrun with Americans on holiday. The Outer Islands, where we hoped to head, were crammed with locals enjoying their Homecoming weekend, a break from their menial jobs in sweatshops and hotels so, between the Yanks and the locals, all the accommodation and transport in the archipelago were booked up.

Certainly there was no prospect of getting transport to or accommodation on San Salvador, where a 3 metre high wooden cross was erected in 1956 as a monument to Columbus' landfall. Nor, it turned out, were we going to have any luck getting to Bimini, just northwest of Nassau, where Gavin Menzies argued in his book that a vast fleet of Chinese junks under the command of Admiral Zheng landed in 1421, 70 years before Columbus' accidental collision with the midriff of the Americas. Menzies has based this startling proposition on the existence, just offshore from Bimini, of a bunch of stones arranged into two regular formations, one shaped like a hockey stick, the other converging with it in a perfectly straight line. His argument is that the stones were a slipway constructed from a mixture of ballast stones and materials quarried by the Chinese to haul up their boats to carry out maintenance. From our perspective, that explanation of the so-called Bimini Road was a bit more credible than the suggestion it was the ancient stairway down to Atlantis.

There was another attraction. Besides Bimini Road, the 16th century Spanish explorer Juan Ponce de Léon — the first of Columbus' crew, as it happens, to sight the North American mainland — recorded Indian testimony that a natural spring on the island was none other than the Fountain of Youth. After 30 hours spent jammed in economy class we all could have done with a bit of that action. But it wasn't to be; there was no room at the Bimini inn.

While we were stewing in the hothouse otherwise known as the Nassau passenger terminal, looking for anything that might give us something to do and somewhere to stay in the Bahamas, Jo got talking to a suave, hustler-like character standing nearby. He was curious about our plans and, on learning we were proposing to go to San Salvador, screwed up his face.

'Dunno why you'd want to go out there. It's a horrible little place, full of mosquitoes,' he said.

Jo told him it was all academic as it looked like we were stuck on Nassau. The bloke then disclosed that he was about to charter a plane to Eleuthera Island (which Jo misheard as 'Urethra Island'), one and a half hours to the east of Nassau, where he 'had a place'. He seemed mildly aghast that she hadn't heard of it. If we wanted to share transport and accommodation we were welcome. It would cost $150 each. Jo accepted on the spot, and Gareth and Dave were introduced to our benefactor, Bob Chappell.

Now Bob was a charmer. While his dark, flowing locks, white suit and chain-smoking seemed out of place in the sweaty precincts of Nassau's airport shed, we were soon to discover just how much at home he was on his tropical island paradise. He clinically negotiated the deal with Jo — no easy task — and within minutes the Cessna 402 with its cargo of Bob and friends plus three Kiwi interlopers was above the Caribbean cays and shoals, making a beeline for its easternmost extremes. This little synchronicity was a promising start to our new adventure.

Eleuthera Island is a stunning sight from the air, a long (176 km), low, thin strip of land curling protectively as though to shield itself from the caprice of the stormy Atlantic. The water to seaward was a deep indigo, contrasting with the azure, coral-mottled shallows to the west — everyone's mental image of a Caribbean atoll. And when we say thin, we mean thin. You could stand in the middle of the island and throw a stone east into the Atlantic then turn around and throw another west into the Caribbean. Indeed, a bridge — once a natural rock arch — is all that holds the island together at one point. It's called the Glass Window, as mariners tossing and heaving on the stormy Atlantic can look right through it into the calm waters of the Caribbean. Because of the shelter it affords so close to the Spanish Main, Eleuthera was once used as a headquarters by those real-life pirates of the Caribbean, Sir Francis Drake and Henry Morgan (no relation, so far as we know).

It turns out that Jimmy Buffett, Elle Macpherson and a fair few other A-listers have properties on Eleuthera. Our unassuming host pointed out a few of their pads on the way from the airstrip to his own, the Rock Sound Club, a resort that had fallen on hard times before he bought it and set about restoring it. Built in the 1920s by the then fourth richest man in the world, aluminium magnate Arthur Vining Davis, the Rock Sound Club had passed through the hands of Juan Trippe, chief executive of Pan Am Airlines, and had hosted such luminaries as Ernest Hemingway, Howard Hughes and assorted British royals. An air of decaying grandeur hung all over. Where tanned, expensively groomed bodies had splashed in the pool, now only mosquito larvae wriggled in the brackish brown waters.

Bob was restoring the place to its former glory, renovating the pavilion, pool and bungalows and buying the surrounding land and subdividing it. He was confident that this once-popular Bahaman Bohemia would once again pump to the rhythms of America's moneyed gentry escaping the rat race for the occasional interlude in Tropicana. There was news of a major resort complex going in further down the atoll so his optimism in returning Rock Sound to its vibrant past may yet be vindicated.

For now, where chandeliers had once dangled, bats hung from the ceilings of the main buildings and the stench of their droppings on the floorboards permeated the rooms rather than the scent of expensive perfumes and rich cigar smoke. The chaises longues of those halcyon days had been smothered by heaps of rotting vegetation. Bob would be a busy boy turning the clock back on this one.

We found boxes containing hundreds of copies of a book named *Secrets of Offshore Tax Havens* in the cottage where we were staying, the author none other than Robert Chappell. Needless to say, Gareth's eyes lit up. He and the charming Mr Chappell sat up debating international investment and the rights and wrongs of tax policy late into the night. Googling our host later, we learned that our Bob had been a notable figure in his own right — or perhaps 'notorious' is the more accurate term. Besides being author of the tax haven book, he was the founder of a Bahaman tax shelter and had been a fugitive from the United States Inland Revenue Service in his time.

Meanwhile, we were waited on hand and foot by Bob's staff, for while it was all a bit run down, the Rock Sound still functioned as a resort. We ate crayfish washed down with champagne and when we returned from swimming, sunbathing and touring Eleuthera in Bob's car the following day we found the beds all made up.

While Christopher Columbus' motive had been to prove Signor Marco Polo had taken the long route to China, his expectations of the New World are obscure. He claimed at various times in his life that his mission was evangelistic, bringing the gospel to the heathen. On the other hand, he persuaded Queen Isabella to make him Admiral of the Ocean Sea and viceroy and governor of any territories he should discover and claim for Spain. He also elicited a guarantee of 10 per cent of any spoils or treasures the trip should uncover and an eighth share of any business enterprises that might subsequently be established by their majesties' subjects in the new lands.

According to the story, Columbus never wavered from believing that the territory he encountered on the far side of the Ocean Sea was China or at least some part of the Indies. When finally he reached the American mainland — the Paria Peninsula, in what is now Venezuela — he is supposed to have believed he was standing on a projecting part of the Asian mainland.

Our flight back to the American mainland took us over the long, linked pair of islands of Bimini and we were able to see the Bimini Road quite clearly in the turquoise water on the ocean side. It's an extraordinary structure. Most experts concede that the symmetry of the blocks, the overall pattern and the presence of stone that could not have originated on Bimini means that it's almost certainly man-made.

We landed at Fort Lauderdale, Florida, for the biking start of our American tour on 17 April and headed down to Miami the following day. Roger flew in and we met him at the airport to break the news to him that our bikes weren't in Miami with us, where they should be. In shades of the start of the Silk Road trip, bureaucracy had held them up in transit and there were rumours that they were on a train somewhere in Alabama. A few frantic phone calls later we learned from a softly spoken woman named Renee that they were due to arrive in Charleston, South Carolina, the following day.

Coincidentally, Charleston was on our list of places to visit — it was the spot where the American Civil War broke out on 12 April 1861 — and it now seemed that our riderless bikes had beaten us to it. We conferred briefly then instructed Renee to ensure the bikes went no further. We were on our way up.

The next day we hired a car and with a GPS jury-rigged on the dashboard, hit the road for the 1000 km drive to Charleston, which took us three days. We spent the first night at pretty Vero Beach, halfway up the dangly bit of land that is Florida, and the second at St Augustine, the site of the oldest permanent European settlement on the North

American continent. The Spanish had made six abortive attempts to get a colony going in North America so when a bunch of Frenchmen managed to set one up at the mouth of St John's River in 1564 the Spanish king, Philip II, wasn't going to stand for it. The following year he sent Pedro Menéndez de Avilés to boot them out. Menéndez arrived off the coast of 'The Land of Flowers' (Florida) on 28 August, the day of the feast of St Augustine. Menéndez dealt to the French in short order and set about building a town that he named after the saint.

Nothing much remains of that original town or its various incarnations up to the 18th century. Buildings fell, burnt or rotted down or were smashed when the British sacked the place in 1702. The only building to survive that wrecking spree was the impressive Castillo San Marcos but there's plenty of other more recent Spanish architecture there and the old part of the city is laid out to a town plan drawn up in the 16th century. The slave market where Africans were bought and sold was pretty much on the spot where Ponce De Léon had earlier landed, still looking for his Fountain of Youth.

We arrived in Charleston on 21 April and the following morning were directed to a warehouse where we saw, with considerable relief, the wooden crates that housed our bikes. We prised them open and checked everything was in working order then began loading our gear. We had far less to carry on this trip than in the wilds of Central Asia on the Silk Road, where we had to be as self-sufficient as possible.

That evening, after a poke about Fort Sumter, which saw some of the first fighting of the Civil War, we found a lovely place to stay about an hour's ride up the coast at Pawleys Island, sandwiched between a huge swamp and a beautiful white-sand beach. In the morning we packed up, consulted our maps, loaded waypoints into our GPS units and fired the bikes up. With a nod to one another we hit the highway, settled into our touring formation and set off to look for America.

COUNTRY ROADS, TAKE ME HOME

As you'd expect of an economic superpower, America is blessed with an incredible roading system. The Interstate highways, wide, straight and finished with a surface Transit New Zealand can only dream of, can take you practically anywhere you want to go with a minimum of fuss and mucking around.

Bugger that, we thought. Fuss and mucking around is what adventure motorcycling is all about. We wanted to get into the backblocks of America, to cut a swathe through the heartland, and the only way to do that was to avoid the major centres of population and take the minor roads. And to find the roads that suited our purposes best we used GPS technology.

Global Positioning by Satellite — GPS — works thanks to a swarm of satellites parked in stationary orbit around the planet, constantly beaming signals to the surface. The

GPS set that you mount in your car, boat, aircraft or cruise missile, and that we mounted on our handlebars, receives these signals. By receiving a signal from at least three of them, identifying the satellites from which they originate and working out its distance from each, the set can pinpoint its own position to within a couple of metres — the wonders of triangulation.

The Garmin StreetPilots we used can not only mark your position on their stored maps but can work out the best route to your destination. You can even tell these amazing little machines how you want to travel — whether you want to get there as fast as possible (whereupon they will plot a course on the Interstates), by taking the shortest route (they will even direct you through lanes and back alleys) or by avoiding major roads. They show the position of gas stations, stores and churches and you can download software for them that will locate scenic, historical and cultural points of interest.

We used GPS far less on our traverse of the Silk Road. Because the mapping of the countries we crossed on that trip is incomplete or inaccurate, we couldn't use most of the whiz-bang features of these units. Instead we used them only for verifying that we were headed in the general direction of China. But in America the mapping is unbelievably detailed — far more detailed, in fact, than the units themselves bargain for. We quickly found that not only could they direct us away from the Interstates and major centres of population and onto secondary roads but there was another class of road again that was beneath the digital dignity of auto-routing. By scanning the little LCD screens of the units for ghostly green lines we could find the roads that were even less travelled, making sure of course that green line eventually joined up with a main road — plenty vanished in the mountains or the desert. These narrow, winding shingle roads, we discovered, pierced the heartland of America.

IN GOD WE TRUST

One thing about Gareth — and he's the first to admit it — is that he can be a little slow to pick up on changes in his environment, particularly when it comes to the people around him. Little cues, the occasional hint, subtleties of body language; they pass him by. It's usually up to Jo, our official Witchfinder-General, to pick up on the little things.

So it was Jo who, in a bar somewhere in Florida in the first few days of the trip, suddenly turned to Roger and said: 'So you believe in God, then?'

Roger jerked his head back in surprise.

'Why are you asking me rather than him?' he replied, nodding at Dave.

'Oh, we know about Dave,' Jo replied. 'I want to know about you.'

Who knows what it was. Perhaps it was the silence from Roger's quarter whenever Gareth snorted at a praise-the-Lord bumper sticker. Perhaps it was the slightly strained smile on his face whenever Gareth made some crack about holy rollers or happy clappies. Perhaps it was the tension in his shoulders whenever Gareth muttered that religion was 'mumbo-jumbo'.

Whatever it was, there were enough clues to alert Jo to the fact that Roger didn't quite seem to be singing from the same page of the hymn book as the rest of us when the subject of religion came up. And, given that one of Gareth's objectives with the Backblocks America tour was to unravel how Christian fanaticism has spread across the so-called home of the secular societies, Roger suddenly found himself as the troupe's apologist for the foible of faith, reminded incessantly by Gareth that America's founding atheists — Thomas Jefferson, Abe Lincoln, Benjamin Franklin and Mark Twain — would not have been impressed by a president performing 'God's work' in Iraq.

Jo is from a fairly traditional Catholic background — all her schooling was at the hands of nuns in Catholic schools in Southland. Her attitude is that spirituality is a positive thing and common to all nations but it has been subverted by power-seekers, with each church, club, clique and creed claiming to have exclusive access to The Truth and a god-given right to persecute the rest. She remembers all too vividly praying that non-Catholics would one day see the light and at the same time reciting over and over that part of the catechism that espoused the Catholic church as the one true church.

Gareth remembers that as a boy he and his friends would pass the kids coming out of the Catholic school down the road and chant, 'Catholic dogs, sit on logs, eating the gutses out of frogs'. He was brought up Anglican long enough to be confirmed but has never had much truck with the church, especially with the typical Anglican strictly-births-deaths-and-marriages observance, the tendency to bend the knee only on ceremonial occasions. For him religious moderates are little more than failed fundamentalists who quarantine praising the Lord to Sundays so it doesn't interfere with their material lives.

Not that he admires full adherence any more. He's an economist after all and the leading lights for economists are reason and intellect. Religion, for Gareth, is a deliberate suspension of the intellect, a decision by otherwise rational people to think logically for six days a week and then flick a switch for the seventh and let rituals of superstition take over, maintain a vain belief in their own eternity, submit comfortably to the will of an all-powerful deity and observe moronic obeisance to the words of scriptures that advocate violence more than they do peace.

So it probably wasn't all that hard for Roger to work out that he was Daniel in the lions' den on this expedition. For Roger, as it turned out, does believe in God. More than that, as he revealed to us that evening over a beer in Florida, he's a Lutheran lay preacher.

As personal disclosures go this was a biggie and all the bigger to be making it now that we were committed to spending the next four months in one another's company. For Gareth, once he'd got over the shock, the revelation presented an opportunity. Having someone along who would push back against his atheist perspective was going to be fun.

Americans will have you believe the country was founded on the principle of religious toleration — or at least the main phase of colonisation was. There wasn't much that was tolerant about the conquistadors who founded St Augustine.

For modern Americans, the sentimental birth of their nation was 11 November 1620. It was on this day that a leaky old windjammer named the *Mayflower* finished her rough crossing of the Atlantic, bringing her complement of passengers to the new land they intended to settle. It had been a rugged trip from England. In all, 102 men, women and children had set out from Plymouth on the *Mayflower* on 6 September. A hundred and three actually reached the New World at Cape Cod, as one of the passengers had given birth en route. Two others dropped their bundles shortly after landfall.

The *Mayflower* immigrants weren't the first to settle North America by any means but the distinctive feature of their colony — and the feature it had in common with much of the subsequent colonisation of America — was that these people had come seeking the freedom to worship however they damn well pleased. They were Puritans, members of the Church of England who thought that there was just too much rank Roman Catholicism surviving in the Anglican liturgy and wanted it further purged. Trouble was, King James I had decided it was job-and-finish on the Protestant Reformation and anyone who didn't agree could just lump it or leave. The king was head of the Church of England and attending Anglican services and muttering the Anglican liturgy was enforced by law. To dispute the way Anglicans did things or even to refuse to go to church would land you in a world of trouble at a time when they were still burning people at the stake, cutting out tongues, slitting nostrils, lopping off ears and pre-emptively curing testicular cancer with a knife.

So you could call them Puritans, you could call them Precisians, but you couldn't call the *Mayflower* crowd stupid. Things were booming in the other English settlements in America, which had been founded in the name of Mammon rather than God. Why not start all over with a nice, clean slate in a territory where the business prospects were good?

Over the next hundred years — some would say three hundred — other religious groups found their way to America, seeking the same freedom to bother God in their own particular way as the *Mayflower* pilgrims had sought. A bunch of Catholics founded Maryland in 1634. (Catholics had blotted their copybook in England under the reign of Bloody Mary Tudor in the late 16th century, when they burnt a bunch of Reforming clergy at the stake for heresy. Consequently, they were personae non grata in England until the Glorious Revolution of 1689.) A bunch of Jews came to the Dutch settlement of New Amsterdam in 1654. They had been getting along fine, minding their own business in the Dutch colony in Brazil until the Portuguese invaded, whereupon they relocated to North America. It was the beginning of a long association of Jews with New Amsterdam, which was renamed New York in 1664 after the British assumed sovereignty. (Wall Street is named for the wall that once surrounded the Dutch colony.)

The first contingent of the Society of Friends — known

to outsiders as Quakers, for the strange, convulsive fits they enter when the spirit of the Lord is upon them — arrived in the 1670s but many more followed once William Penn founded Pennsylvania in 1682. Penn was a Quaker and had been persecuted in his native England for his beliefs. Fortunately for him, his family was owed a large debt by the English crown and Charles II granted him the entirety of what is now the state of Pennsylvania in settlement. So he founded Pennsylvania as an asylum for Quakers and other groups persecuted for their religion. One of these, who wasted little time in making themselves at home, were the Mennonites, the principally German followers of 15th century seer Menno Simons. Due to linguistic confusion, the Germans who settled in Pennsylvania, the Pennsylvania Deutsch, became known as the Pennsylvania Dutch and are referred to as such to this day.

Many of these sects had suffered persecution at the hands of others, especially by the established or dominant religions in their country of origin. They were understandably all in favour of religious toleration. Roger Williams, for example, welcomed all religious comers to the utopia of toleration he founded on Rhode Island, no matter how wacky their beliefs seemed, because he believed 'forced worship stinks in God's nostrils'.

Yet toleration was not the universal creed among the various sects, many of whom — same old story — were convinced that they were right about religion and everyone else was wrong.

Many of the founders of the 'plantations of religion' that were created in America had their own established churches and so did the states that succeeded them. These would have been happy for there to be an established Church of America after independence had been won from England but there was fat chance all these groups would agree on what kind of church to establish. Some of them even interpreted the War of Independence as a struggle against the corrupt Church of England, with victory being God's signal to establish the true church in the New World. Independence from England was all a little bit awkward for American Anglicans because the King of England was the head of their church. Shaking off the yoke of the English monarchy left them with a headless church.

Those who drafted the United States Constitution in 1787 were smart enough to realise that any move to create a federal church was a recipe for deep division and quite probably civil war. The constitution therefore mostly sidestepped religion.

A couple of years later, however, under pressure to make some kind of determination on the subject of religion, the First Amendment to the constitution was enacted, which forbade federal and state moves to establish a church and guaranteed Americans the freedom to worship as they saw fit. It was an attempt to establish the principle of religious toleration, instead of a single church.

The United States may be a secular country by virtue of this amendment to the constitution but it's impossible not to feel you're in a fanatically religious country when you're riding on through. There's lately been another flurry of revivalism, with endless petitions presented to Congress since 1995 to allow preachers into schools and for happy-clappy bonding classes to be part of the curriculum. These have yet to succeed but there is definite religious creep in the secular institutions of American democracy. Thanks to recent court action, this fundamentalist Christian revival in America has won the right to teach creationism in junior school before the curriculum of high school can 'pollute' young minds with talk of evolution. Thanks to a 2001 Supreme Court ruling, Bible classes are being held in the classroom (by the same teacher that has the kids all day) straight after the bell rings for end of school.

We heard about all this in action when we were in Moab, Utah. A local school had surrendered its right to refuse some Christian mystic running his 'Good News' club for students in the classroom after school because he had threatened to use a well-heeled Christian activist lobby, The American Center for Law and Justice, to fight the school for as long and as much as it took to win. Moab is a small district, and as the school president pointed out, 'We don't have the funds to go all the way to the Supreme Court.'

This religious revivalism and move to confront the First Amendment seems to be an escalation of a trend that has been underway in the United States for 150 years. The drama in Moab is just one instance of how the constitutional guarantees of a secular state are under attack in contemporary America.

Another celebrated case occurred in 2004 when a 12 year old in Ohio wore a T-shirt to school declaring: 'Homosexuality is a sin, Islam is a lie, abortion is murder. Some issues are just black and white.' He beat a legal challenge from his school on the grounds of freedom to express religious conviction. He would have lost if he had claimed freedom of speech because such freedom doesn't permit expressions of hate — in the United States you can only get away with hate speech if it's based on your religion.

It's a shock to the system going to heavily religious America from New Zealand, which would have to be one of the most secular societies in the world. But it pays to remember that it's not that long ago we couldn't shop, drink or gamble on Sundays. Even the screening of television advertising was forbidden on the sabbath. Our colonial forebears feared the Lord with the best of them but somehow we've moved on from all that. We've turned our back on it — as a society we're not far from the pure, secular notion that religion is an invention of man, designed primarily to control the lives of other men and women.

From what we saw, America has abandoned this journey, preferring to backtrack on any tentative steps its founders may have taken toward religious neutrality. Nowadays religious fundamentalism rules. Practically every vehicle on the road sports a bumper sticker with a message along the lines of 'God Bless America' or 'God Keep Our Troops Safe' or 'God Bring Otis Home Soon'. And motels, gas stations and shops display similar messages on their signage: 'Guest Laundry, Outdoor Hot Tub, God Bless America'; 'Cheap Gas, Lord Look After Our Boys in Iraq'.

Our very first Sunday in America saw us cruising along a dusty back road in South Carolina, inland from Pawleys Island and bound for the little town of Wilson, across the border in North Carolina. We traversed one section of road,

Above: *It's not all beaches and Bacardis in the Bahamas.*

Below: *The team ready to ride.*

Left: *Trading places — the slave mart at St Augustine.*

Below: *Roger and Gareth's religious debate carrying on in suitable surrounds — St Augustine, Florida.*

Left: *Bloody Jap car is too tight for this good ol' American boy.*

Above: *Amish folk — Mesopotamia, Ohio.*

Left: *Follow me little ducklings — Mesopotamia, Ohio.*

Above: *Taking to the highway — Arizona.*

Below: *Easyrider gutsas — bits of bikes that failed to tame the Dragon.*

Above: *Cara-liner — North Carolina.*

Below: *A common scene — trailer home, satellite dish and a pick-up truck.*

Above: *Martin Luther King's Ebenezer Baptist Church — Auburn Ave, Atlanta.*

Above: *Scene of Dr King's murder — Memphis.*

Below: *Lost again!*

Above: *Davy Crockett's cabin, Tennessee.*

Below: *Elvis' birthplace — Tupelo, Mississippi.*

Above: *Elvis' original cellphone — Graceland, Memphis.*

Below: *Edmund Pettus Bridge, Selma, Alabama — scene of the Bloody Sunday police attack on civil rights marchers in March 1965.*

which must have been 80 km long, where there wasn't a shop or a service station to be seen. Every couple of kilometres though there were great barn-like buildings set amid well-tended, park-like grounds, with their carparks jammed with SUVs and farm vehicles glittering in the sun. There were crosses on the walls and roofs and the doors of these buildings and they were locked and their curtains drawn. Who knows what was going on inside?

Gareth thought Roger might have an idea but Roger knows when someone's having a go at him. He just smiled tightly and suggested that the number of churches was testimony to the weight of numbers — the American people voting for the Lord with the bums that they park on pews.

On the evening of Saturday 13 May we were in a pretty rough pub in Vicksburg, Mississippi, a town renowned as the site of one of the sharpest battles of the Civil War, when the notion of actually attending a church service was floated. Gareth said he'd sit this one out but Dave and Jo were game. We had no way of knowing the times of services or the best church to attend so it occurred to us to ask at the bar.

The barmaid looked like pure, Southern white trash but, if it struck her that there was something strange about our question, she gave nothing away.

'Hey, Ned,' she yelled across the bar.

A hairy, heavy-set, tattooed brute of a man looked up from his Budweiser.

'What time's church over your way?'

'Well,' he replied. 'There's a service at seven and another at nine ...'

'You don't want to go there,' piped up someone else, pretty

closely resembling a Hell's Angel. 'Preacher's boring.'

Most of the clientele of the bar — rugged, scarred and scary-looking as they were — began debating the relative merits of the churches of Vicksburg for our benefit. When eventually a consensus was reached on which church we should attend, attention turned to the service times. The bar backed onto another and the barmaid came through from the other side.

'We got all the times right here,' she said. 'Under the counter.'

A piece of paper was produced that listed the times of all the services at the appointed church.

So Dave, Roger and Jo all put on our Sunday best — that is, their only set of off-bike threads — and took off to church the next morning. It was quite an experience. Pastor Mike, a biker as it turned out and every inch the slick televangelist complete with expensive grooming and petite blonde wife, welcomed them as 'our friends all the way from New Zealand' and members of the congregation shook their hands. It was hard to tell what denomination the service was but it was refreshingly multicultural and there was lots of singing — courtesy of a 'Southern Choir' — and praying. They each got presented with a souvenir cup at the end of the service and were told that the best wishes and prayers of the biker-loving congregation went with them.

Never mind America, we were having our own problems with religious toleration. Now that Roger was out of the closet — or perhaps that should be the confessional — he and Gareth were already well into a verbal sparring match that lasted right across America.

Roger started to educate Gareth on how his Lutheran church had the most followers of all Protestants and that it had been created in the Reformation during a revolt against Rome's political control over Europe through the Catholic church. Martin Luther was the hero of the Reformation, he instructed Gareth.

'That's a name you obviously have some familiarity with,' he said, 'from your knowledge of the civil rights movement in Alabama.'

Roger's objective was clear — to make Gareth connect his admiration for Martin Luther King with his namesake, the founder of the Lutheran church.

Gareth needed a counterpunch and it wasn't long coming. At his suggestion we headed north from the Shenandoah River and up across Pennsylvania and into northern Ohio, pretty well to Lake Erie and the town of Parkman and a village just outside of that called Mesopotamia. Here, F250 pickups and 400-horsepower Chevy Silverados have to share the road with the single-horsepower buggies of the Amish. It was a hell of a long way to ride to make a theological point but Gareth duly made it: that the Amish had broken away from the Lutherans for exactly the same reasons the Lutherans had broken away from the Catholics, and the primitive Amish lifestyle was what real seperation from worldly affairs looked like.

Standing at the bottom of the Grand Canyon, which had so obviously been scoured out of the rock over millions of years by the slow grinding of the Colorado River, Gareth turned to Roger.

'Still believe all this was created in 4004 BC?' he said.

Roger nodded.

Roger retaliated later in New Mexico, when he noticed Gareth staring gobsmacked at the great fluted and vaulted domes of the Big Room in the Carlsbad Caverns cave system.

'You like that, Gareth?' he said. 'Pretty, isn't it? It's God's work.'

You could just about see the steam coming out Gareth's ears.

Meanwhile, we were seeing signs of the religious fervour of the American people everywhere. People were always saying 'God bless you' in a way that is strikingly similar to 'Salaam aleikum' in Muslim countries. Jo stopped to fill up at a gas station and got talking to a big, whiskery bloke in the forecourt who asked where we'd been and where we were heading. He listened as she explained the World by Bike agenda and the American itinerary in particular then, to her alarm, he lurched forward and wrapped her in a great bear hug.

'May the good Lord keep you safe, little lady,' he said hoarsely.

Only in America, she thought.

And you could trust Dave to find a way to work all that piety in our favour. When we were chewing the fat with strangers he took to saying, as though he were musing out loud: 'Ah, the good people in the last state were so generous. Everywhere we went people were inviting us into their homes and giving us a meal. Wonderful folk. Really wonderful.'

There would be a moment's pause and then his audience

would start falling over themselves to offer dinner and accommodation to keep up with the godly Joneses in the last state. It would be up to the rest of us to put a stop to it.

'No, Dave. You've already had a good meal. You don't need another one.'

All the way Gareth kept on at Roger.

'It's pretty easy to see how the mullahs and ayatollahs get everyone behind them,' he'd say. 'All you need is a bunch of fear-ridden servile sheep like the religious nutters you've got over here.'

And Roger kept giving as good as he got. One of the projects we were working on while in America was to seek out worthy aid operations to fund through our new charitable trust. It was pretty conspicuous that a lot of the people involved in this work were Christians, motivated by their beliefs to do amazing work.

Roger kept pointing this out to Gareth.

'You admire all these people for the good they do, Gareth,' he'd say. 'How is it you can dismiss them as brainless sheep at the same time?'

Then there was always Martin Luther King.

'Just a mindless follower too Gareth, was he?'

Most European countries either have an established church or belong to some denomination or other 'by confession'. Spain and Italy are Catholic countries, for example, because their rulers consider themselves to be good subjects of the Pope. Queen Elizabeth II is head of the Church of England. In each case, the church is in a privileged position over its rivals and, even where the state doesn't directly fund the church (as it does in Spain), gathering congregations and extracting tithes from them is not a problem.

In America the government gives churches and religious organisations a few breaks: it's easier to get zoning permission to set up a church than a panelbeating business, churches get an easier ride when it comes to providing parking for the SUVs in which the faithful flock to the door and the property on which churches are built is free of taxes. But that's as far as state assistance goes. Anything further, such as opening local government meetings with a prayer or even putting up a Christmas tree in the lobby of a government building, has to be done very carefully. You can argue the prayer took place in everyone's personal time before the meeting opened and you'll get away with it. The Christmas tree is going to be harder to defend. For a branch of local, state or federal government to display the emblem of any religion is a breach of the First Amendment, which guarantees the separation of church and state.

It's often been noted that as the standard of living of a country rises, religious backsliding gathers momentum. It stands to reason that the happier you are with your lot in this life, the less urgent it seems to secure a stake in the next. So it was in early America, where the piety of the pilgrims was replaced by the rather more lukewarm complacency of prospering farmers.

But an odd thing happened in the 19th century. The slow ebb of religious fervour was reversed and an explosion of zeal occurred in the 1840s that is often referred to as the 'Great Awakening.'

This has been attributed to the First Amendment. The decision not to establish any one church in America exposed the many churches to market forces — since no one religious group could rely on state patronage and funding they all had to rely on good old-fashioned marketing instead. The Great Awakening was the beginning of evangelism — the aggressive selling of your church's religious message to the people.

Charismatic Christianity — otherwise known as the 'happy clappy' school — had its roots here. Instead of mumbling in Latin and delivering long, boring homilies and sermons, the pressure was on parsons and pastors to sex up the message with singalongs, high-flown oratory and other tricks of the trade to ignite mass hysteria.

That's why, when you drive through the outskirts of a town in South Carolina, you'll see a big gaudy plastic sign for Wendy's, another for McDonald's, another for KFC and another for Burger King. In the middle of them, there'll be a big gaudy plastic sign advertising The Revival Centre or some such evangelistic operation. It's because they're all in the same business. The food outlets sell junk food for the body; the churches peddle fast food for the soul.

This marketing acumen is almost certainly what accounts for the extraordinary religiousness of the American people today. Only five per cent of New Zealanders are regular churchgoers. In America that figure is a whopping 47 per cent and in parts — such as in the South and especially, as far as we could tell, in the Carolinas, with their ecclesiastical strip-malls — it must be nearer 80 per cent of the population.

It's also what accounts for the creeping mingling of church

and state in America since the end of the 1970s. While the First Amendment was designed to prevent the state meddling in worship, those who drafted it didn't really see a problem with worshippers meddling with the affairs of state.

Before we left for America, Gareth read a book by two English journalists who had studied the Neo-Conservative movement in America. *The Right Nation*, by John Micklethwait and Adrian Wooldridge, documented among other scary things the penetration of American politics by the conservative, fundamentalist religious lobby. In the last few elections, culminating in the most recent election of George Dubya Bush, this well-organised, motivated and mobilised contingent has pulled the rhetoric of both the Republicans and the Democrats to the right on issues such as abortion and homosexuality. And the Republican party agenda has been all but captured by religious conservatism, to the extent that candidates for Republican party office feel obliged to beat a path — and be seen to be beating a path — to the doors of a fundamentalist lobby group called Focus on the Family, based in Colorado. As a measure of how powerful this group is and how great their following has become, their Colorado Springs 'campus' has its own freeway exit and its own zip code.

The hardest part for Gareth was containing his opinions on all this, which in the end he had to do in the interests of preserving harmony within the group. To say what he really thought of this state of affairs risked badly offending Roger.

But by the end of the trip the strain was almost too great. By now there was an edge to his jibes. Roger is an immensely physically strong man and was fond of showing it by sitting on the floor with his legs out in front of him, resting his hands on the floor to either side and lifting himself off the floor with his knuckles, still with his legs stretched out. It was a pretty impressive feat of gymnastics.

'Just like a monkey!' Gareth crowed when he saw it. 'You're sure you don't believe in evolution?'

TO HAVE
AND HAVE NOT

Among the many emails that we received before and during our trip was one from a bloke who specialises in importing wood-turning equipment into North America from New Zealand. A biker and a BMW owner, Ernie had followed our Silk Road journey with interest and, hearing we were travelling to America, he contacted us and offered to guide us through the Amish farming community in rural Ohio.

That looked interesting, we thought — especially Gareth, who spied an opportunity to further his end of the debate with Roger on the subject of religion. So we made a detour from our traverse of the Appalachians at Warrenton, a little to the southeast of Washington, and headed north by west for southern Pennsylvania and Ohio. The temperature dropped appreciably and the trees were yet to get their spring foliage as we rode north to Parkman, Ohio, almost at the shores of

Lake Erie, where we met Ernie and bunch of members of the local BMW owners club.

‗‗‗‗‗‗‗‗‗‗‗‗‗‗‗‗‗‗‗‗‗‗‗‗‗‗

The Amish are a sect who broke away from the Mennonites, who had earlier broken away from the Lutherans. Menno Simons had started out as a Catholic but became a follower of Luther until ultimately he got frustrated at the Lutheran Reformation too, which he regarded as a job half done. The main sticking point was the rite of baptism, which most radical reformers thought should be performed on consenting adults rather than infants. Because they had a tendency to baptise believers who had already been baptised by the Catholic or Lutheran churches, the Mennonites, in common with other radicals, became known as 'anabaptists' ('ana-' meaning 'twice' or 'again'). The other sticking point was religious toleration. Lutheran Germany was as anxious to enforce its orthodoxy as Rome ever was and the Mennonites found themselves being hounded by Catholics and Protestants alike. In the face of persecution they spread out over Europe and as far afield as Russia and South and North America.

'Your lot told the Pope to naff off on the question of mixing church and state,' Gareth pointed out to Roger. 'Well, the Mennonites and the Amish told your lot to do the same for exactly the same reason. And in so-called secular America these guys seem to be the only ones left who can keep their church out of politics.'

Smiling his turn-the-other-cheek smile, Roger resisted engaging Gareth and having his Lutherans labelled fundamentalists again.

A little more than a hundred years after Menno seceded from Lutheranism, a Swiss Mennonite named Jacob Amman grew discontented with what he regarded as the corrupt and licentious practices of that sect. His followers established a breakaway sect, the Amish, who were quick to shift to Pennsylvania in the early 18th century to escape the inevitable persecution they suffered in Europe and take advantage of the newly established utopia of religious tolerance.

Like the Mennonites, the Amish believe in adult baptism and the virtues of obedience to authority, humility, thrift and simplicity. Both the Mennonites and the Amish take 'simplicity' to mean living a lifestyle quarantined from the materialism of the modern world, although the Mennonites are a little more practical about it than the Amish. You'll see Mennonites driving pickups but you'll never see an Amish driving a vehicle with any more horsepower than he can yoke to it. The simple lives of both sects reflect the role they believe religious virtue ought to play in their day-to-day lives. Not for them confining their religiosity to tokenism on Sundays. Unlike the Mennonites, the Amish don't vote, which reveals the depth of their conviction that the godly ought not to be beholden to any outside super-authority, be it the state or some elaborate church hierarchy. The Amish don't have churches — the bishop moves about, holding the Sunday service in their homes. Family is paramount.

The difference of opinion between the two sects arose over the degree to which their communities ought to remain separate from the rest of us sinners. The Amish are stricter on the subject of discipline. If you transgress you're liable to be excommunicated and shunned. The rest of the community is obliged to cut all contact with a member so treated even if they're close family.

Membership of the sect is supposed to be a matter of informed consent and thus many Amish communities allow their young people to indulge in a period of 'rumspringa' ('running around' in Old German), when they are permitted to give the outside world and all its vices a go. If at the end of this period they choose to remain within the sect, they're baptised. If not, they're cast out and shunned.

The Amish around Parkman live alongside but separate from the rest of the local community, with whom we found they had a kind of schizophrenic relationship. On the one hand, the locals seemed to resent the willpower the Amish exercised to maintain their separation, their refusal to 'conform' to good-ole-boy USA. On the other hand they were not only valued for the tourist dollars they pulled into the community but also admired for their work ethic and impeccable honesty. Those who have hired them justly reckon them to be the best employees in America.

One of the first indications that you're in Amish country is the road signs warning motorists to beware of horse-drawn traffic, and it didn't take us long before we saw carriages and carts in action, driven by bearded men in blue cotton shirts, jeans and broad-brimmed straw hats. The women wore flowing blue smocks with long sleeves and skirts and the inevitable head covering, a black bonnet. We saw fields being worked with ploughs drawn by oxen and men prodding at the soil with a variety of traditional hand tools.

We stopped alongside one hitching rail in Mesopotamia where there were a few Amish hot rods parked — Amish central, as it seemed — just in time for a tidy little black 'station wagon' to draw up and a young Amish dude to tether his horse and unload his three kids from the back. The kids made straight for Dave in his space suit. We got talking to dad, whose name was Bill. He looked no more than 35 but had eight children, four boys and four girls. Bill and all the Amish we talked to were polite and mildly interested in our trip but they were aloof with it and wasted no time in getting about their business as soon as they judged the pleasantries were through.

Dark came early and frost settled on the barren fields and we finished off the day as guests of Ernie and Susan, who treated us to a beautiful rosemary-seasoned pork roast, followed by a local specialty, yellow cake, a kind of pineapple cake.

On the way to visit the Amish, we'd passed through Pittsburgh, Pennsylvania, where the entire city is a wireless internet hot-spot, free to all. Earlier in the trip we'd visited Cape Canaveral, from which the lunar landing missions were launched, arguably one of the high points of technological ingenuity. You have to admire the Amish and the courage of their convictions for living the way they do in the midst of a society that is defined by its technological prowess and by consumption and materialism. It makes a refreshing change from standard-issue American fundamentalism, where it's OK to do dog-eat-dog capitalism all week and then to pay lip service to the Christian virtues of neighbourliness, humility and thrift on Sundays. For the Amish it's a full-time commitment. They don't use cars, computers, dishwashers, microwaves and the assorted paraphernalia that we regard as essential to our everyday lives. A community might have a telephone but individual families don't. They don't use cameras and they're not anxious to have their picture taken, as to do so is evidence of ungodly vanity. And despite what we might think, given how important our gadgets are to us, they get along pretty well.

They're not without their problems though. The children we saw were mostly wearing thick glasses; short-sightedness is just one of the congenital disorders rife within their very limited gene pool. After all, it's not as if outsiders are flocking to join up. That their children's education ends in the eighth grade at age 13 would, to the rest of us, seem to destine them to an ignorant funk. But hey, who's to say a traditional, simple life is inferior?

AMERICA IN BLACK AND WHITE

I
t doesn't take you long to work out in what esteem they hold the great civil rights campaigner and martyr Martin Luther King Jr in his hometown of Atlanta, Georgia.

We knew there was a centre dedicated to his memory somewhere around and we wanted to pay a visit. But just try finding it in the see-the-sights brochures they give you at your motel.

If you've got a day to spare in Atlanta, the good folks at the tourism and publicity department recommend you spend it touring the Coca-Cola factory and squeezing in a poke about at the headquarters of CNN. If you've got two days, you'd do well to spend the second at the famous Atlanta Aquarium. If you've got three, why, there's the Jimmy Carter Library and the local Hard Rock Cafe. If you're so fortunate as to have a fourth day to kill, then there's the Botanical Gardens and the Museum of Natural History for your delight and edification.

When we enquired about the Martin Luther King Centre, the locals were mildly put out at our interest. Several indicated it was in a bad neighbourhood — not really somewhere you'd send visitors you were trying to impress. Why didn't we go see the Coke factory? One (white) taxi driver gave us what is likely to be a truer indication of the reason it's so tucked away and neglected.

'Now why the hell would you want to go there?' he drawled. 'All that crap, it's just ancient history.'

In a sense he's right. Racism has a long, distinguished history in America. We'd already come into contact with 'all that crap' on our way up from our landfall at Fort Lauderdale through the Carolinas to Virginia. While we were at the slave auction house in St Augustine Jo fell into conversation with a black Southern mama selling Chinese-made trinkets and asked her about the state of race relations in America. Once she'd got over her surprise at being asked such a frank question, let alone by a white person, she proceeded to deliver our first lesson on the persistence of bigotry, inequality and the oppression of African Americans. She most certainly did not feel equal, she told us — just look at the terrible time her kids were having in the education system, turned away from all of the better schools on the flimsiest of pretexts.

A few hours' ride north of there, across the border in Virginia, we took a vehicular ferry named the *Pocahontas* across the James River and visited Jamestown, which is the site of the first permanent English settlement in North America. In 1607 a hundred or so Englishmen settled on a swampy island in the lower reaches of the river, 70-odd kilometres from where it empties into Chesapeake Bay. It was the eighteenth British attempt to settle America, 45 years after the Spanish had founded St Augustine.

That's one of Jamestown's claims to fame. The other is that it was here in 1619 that the first African slaves sold on the North American mainland changed hands. John Rolfe, Virginia's first tobacco magnate — and incidentally the man who married the real-life Indian princess Pocahontas — reported in a letter that a Dutch man-of-war had exchanged 'twenty and odd' Africans for provisions in August that year. These unfortunates were part of a consignment of 100-odd men and women kidnapped by the Portuguese in the course of their war against the inhabitants of what is now Angola. They were bound for Veracruz in Mexico and lives of servitude in the plantations of the Spanish New World, until fate intervened in the shape of the Dutch *White Lion* and the English *Treasurer*, which sacked the Portuguese vessel and stole her living cargo. The English vessel traded her share in Bermuda. The Dutchman's 'twenty and odd' became the first of about 650,000 Africans sold into slavery in North America over the course of the next 150 years or so. So just like Columbus these wretched unfortunates — the vanguard of the African American population — arrived in their 'New World' quite by accident.

If you want to make fine distinctions, the first slaves weren't really slaves. They were 'indentured servants', technically in the same position as thousands of poor Englishmen and women who worked the Virginia tobacco plantations. The first African to be officially enslaved for life was one John

Punch, an indentured labourer who received his life term of servitude as a punishment for running away in 1640. The slave trade as most people think of it — the abduction of men, women and children from their African homelands and their sale in the stockyards of the American south — didn't get fully underway until the 1680s, when the labour-hungry cotton and tobacco plantations were reaching maturity.

The heyday of slavery had passed by the time it was proposed to abolish the trade in the 1800s. But they were a little touchy about the subject down South and, when the emancipation movement threatened to get the upper hand, the southern states seceded and unified into the Confederacy. Fort Sumter, the stone fortress that covers a wee island at the mouth of the Charleston Harbour, is now a national monument. It's here where the first shots of what became the American Civil War were fired in April 1861, when the Confederates shelled into submission a bunch of Union troops who had holed up there. Our nosey around there revealed clearly visible damage inflicted by the bombardment, including a cannonball still lodged in the weathered masonry.

As everyone knows, the Union won the Civil War, the South was defeated and emancipation duly happened, with the 13th Amendment to the United States constitution passed in 1865, abolishing trading and owning slaves.

The southern states weren't exactly delighted at the outcome. They obeyed the letter of the new law but crapped on its spirit. Most introduced Black Codes, which conferred a raft of new rights upon their dusky citizens — just fewer rights than whites enjoyed. And after 1877, when the Supreme Court declared a Civil Rights Bill unconstitutional, most southern states were quick to enact 'Jim Crow laws' (named after a popular song of 1828 called *Jump Jim Crow* that introduced the term to the lexicon as a derogatory term for the former slaves). Even a century later, in 1955, Rosa Parks was to create a storm by daring to defy the petty apartheid rules that separated whites from blacks when travelling on the buses of the South. It was a reminder that the sexual segregation on buses in Iran we had experienced just a year ago on our Silk Road trip wasn't such a distant memory for the Land of the Free.

In most places in the American South, strict segregation of the races was enforced in every aspect of daily life and blacks were forbidden to vote. But even their legally entrenched position of superiority didn't entirely placate the hatred of the southern bigots — there were more than 3600 lynchings of black men and women between 1877 and World War I.

Gareth grew up at the time America was relitigating the Civil War in the 1960s civil rights movement. He became caught up in his sister's enthusiasm for Martin Luther King Jr when she was researching a sixth-form speech about him — enough to be deeply shocked when he heard one day at school that the charismatic young preacher had been shot dead.

We caught buses in Atlanta — our first day off the bikes since we began the trip — to the memorial site in Auburn

Avenue where King was born and to the Ebenezer Baptist Church where he preached, as did his father before him. The original red-brick church is now a memorial to him and a new church stands across the road. We sat in a pew in the old building and listened to recordings of King's speeches. It was a moving experience — particularly the last speech he gave, in which he expressed his confidence that African Americans would achieve equality with their white oppressors but warned his audience that he might not be there to celebrate the day with them. It seemed he'd already received death threats. It made the hair on the back of our necks stand up to hear his words, considering the tragic end suffered not only by King but also by his mother, Alberta, who was shot by a gun-toting loony while praying in the same church just six years after her son's assassination.

We joined a tour that began at the Auburn Fire Station, the first in America to employ a racially integrated firefighting force, which conducted us around the house in which the civil rights firebrand was born and grew up. It was a pleasant two-storey wooden affair, not unlike the kind of thing you'd see in Wellington's Mt Victoria or in the older parts of Dunedin, with a back yard just about big enough to play baseball in. It was flanked by equally comfortable-looking houses of the same era and across the road there were bigger, flasher houses still. It wasn't exactly a ghetto. King's house is protected and dedicated to his memory.

Down the road is the Martin Luther King Jr Memorial Center (the King Center), with an entrance flanked by impressive bronze statues of Mahatma Gandhi and, holding an infant aloft, Kunta Kinte, the principal character of Alex

Haley's epic novel about the African American experience, *Roots*.

King was born in 1929 and, after graduating with a doctorate in theology, he followed in the footsteps of his father, a Baptist preacher. He first came to national prominence in 1955 when his organisation, the Southern Christian Leadership Conference, instigated a boycott of the buses in Montgomery, Alabama, where young black seamstress Rosa Parks had been arrested for refusing to give up her seat on a bus to a white man, as state law then demanded. The boycott lasted 382 days and ended when the Supreme Court ruled that racial discrimination on public transport was illegal.

King became the figurehead of the national civil rights movement, leading the march on Washington that culminated in his 'I have a dream' speech before the Lincoln Memorial in 1963, and in the process becoming the target of the fear and loathing of American bigots everywhere. President Lyndon Johnson introduced a Civil Rights Act in 1964, effectively making racial discrimination illegal. That didn't go down so well in the South. When 600 marchers headed out of the town of Selma bound for the Alabama state Capitol in Montgomery on 7 March 1965, they were set upon by a mob as they crossed the Edmund Pettus Bridge. Mounted police arrived, jostled the vigilantes aside — and took over the bashing of the marchers with billy clubs and jackboots. The event became known as 'Bloody Sunday' and was a watershed in the civil rights movement. King led another march to the Selma bridge later that month and on to Montgomery. By the time they arrived they were 25,000 strong and their cause had become national. Five months later, Lyndon Johnson passed an act that gave voting rights to black Americans, a hundred years after slavery was abolished.

We read all about this stuff at the King Center, where there was a range of exhibits setting out America's chequered past. Outside, set in the middle of a calm, reflective pool, was a stone marking the spot King is interred. His wife, Coretta, who founded the King Center is buried nearby.

A couple of days later we visited the Lorraine Motel in Memphis, Tennessee, where at 6.01 pm on 4 April 1968 a rifle shot to the throat ended King's life. As with the assassination of John F. Kennedy, the official explanation — that King was shot by a lone white gunman, James Earl Ray, from a nearby apartment block — is widely doubted and a conspiracy theory stretches into the shadier reaches of the corridors of power. The Lorraine Motel too is preserved as a monument. They've even restored a Cadillac coupe identical to King's and parked it permanently where his was parked on that fateful evening.

It was in the carpark of the motel that Jo received yet another perspective on the screwed-up perceptions that America's racial discord has produced. She got into conversation with the attendant, a black chap, who needed little encouragement to launch into a tirade about how hard done by his people were, with difficulties still rife in access to quality schools, jobs and welfare. In an effort to understand the nature of the beast, Jo threw out a tester.

'What,' she asked, 'would happen if your son brought home a white girl and told you he was going to marry her?'

Well, you'd think she'd set his pants on fire. His indignation was ignited and he reverted to biblical references to validate his view that it would be totally wrong, that God didn't mean the races to mix and there would be hell to pay in the family. Yes indeed, the colour issue mixed with America's revived religious fundamentalism is a potent cocktail indeed.

From Tennessee we cruised south into Alabama and made a side-trip to Selma, about 60 km outside Montgomery, to have a look at the Edmund Pettus Bridge, part of a history trail administered by the National Parks Service commemorating the civil rights movement and Bloody Sunday.

The bridge is still in service in its original condition, albeit somewhat depreciated. Those newsreel scenes of black men, women and children solemnly marching over the humped bridge, lawfully keeping to the footpath, only to be charged by mounted state police wielding clubs and firing tear gas, resonated sickeningly as we stood by the bridge and remembered.

Selma remains a 70 per cent black city with a third of the people living below the poverty line. It certainly struck us as drab, with the streets hosting plenty of kerb-sitters with little else to do.

We all found the King Centre to be an intensely moving experience but we were among the very few getting it. We were the only white folks and were sharing the centre with a busload of black schoolchildren. The rest of Atlanta's visitors, we gathered, were queuing up at the Coke factory and CNN. And that's the problem — far from being ancient history that Americans had put behind them when they realised King's dream, racism is alive and kicking in the Land of the Free.

The indifference among Atlantans to King and the civil rights movement is among its more benign manifestations. For instance, when we were riding in the Appalachians, people often asked us where we were heading next. When we told them we were keen to look in on New Orleans, they screwed up their faces.

'Now, why the hell would y'all wanna go there?' people asked. 'N'awlins is the toilet of America and the Lord done flushed it.'

We heard this line — that New Orleans is the toilet bowl of America and stinks accordingly — from several people, including a man in an Appalachian town who could have stepped straight from the movie set of that hillbilly classic *Deliverance* and rejoiced in the name Randy Gums. We kid you not — and his sister's name was Fanny!

We approached New Orleans along long, straight roads over the plains inland from the Gulf of Mexico — the flood plains of the Mississippi Delta. The city is a good way inland but is backed by the saltwater Lake Pontchartrain and kept dry by an immense system of levees, spillways and mighty pumps. People of the Lord's Toilet school shook their heads and wondered aloud for our benefit why anyone would want to live beneath sea level, relying on a few pumps and heaps of dirt to keep their heads above water — as though most of the population of the Netherlands didn't do exactly that.

As we neared the city we began to see mounds of rubbish piled up at the roadsides but it didn't occur to us right away that these were the first indications of the devastating floods that hit this area at the height of the hurricane in August 2005. For while New Orleans used to be connected solely with jazz, bourbon and the Mardi Gras, it is now indelibly associated with the name Katrina.

'Hurricane' is the American term for a tropical cyclone, an intense storm characterised by winds of more than 119 km/h. There's a scale of intensity, with Category 1 the lowest and Category 5 the highest. A Category 1 hurricane will mess up your garden and find you out if your roofing iron isn't secure or your mooring lines are dodgy. Category 5 storms pack winds in excess of 249 km/h and are capable of tearing well-constructed buildings apart.

People who know will tell you that hurricanes can do damage in three ways — with winds, obviously, of unimaginably destructive force, with devastating rainfall and, for areas adjacent to a coast, with storm surges. Storm surge is the consequence of the winds within a cyclone creating a bulge in the ocean that is further inflamed by the low barometric pressure at the cyclone's eye. End result: a kind of king tide, often metres above the usual tidal average and aggravated by a wind-driven swell as well.

That's basically the story of Hurricane Katrina and New Orleans. Katrina was one of the most powerful storms of an already freakish hurricane season; at Category 4 it was right up there nudging the 'perfect storm' of Category 5. It packed winds circulating close to the top speed of Jo's Ducati when it made landfall up the coast from New Orleans and at its peak the storm surge along the Louisiana coast was estimated to be 8.2 m high. The levees protecting New Orleans were breached in several places and the city was inundated.

You'd think that in one of the most affluent countries in the world the areas prone to cyclone damage would have their shit together, planning-wise. It had long been feared that a direct hit by a storm of any decent proportion would devastate New Orleans, so evacuation plans were in place all right. But it turned out that no one had thought to check for bugs — such as the fact that every rest home in the city planned to use the same buses to get their residents out, that the biggest long-distance passenger carriers, Greyhound buses and Amtrak trains, would cancel services before the storm hit to minimise their risk, and the city's infrastructure just couldn't cope with the sheer number of gas-guzzling SUVs that would line up for gas and try to get the hell out on the freeway all at once. Thus, when the evacuation order came, marking the largest movement of human beings on the North American mainland since the Oklahoma Dustbowl of the 1930s, the roads choked, the gas ran out, the train system broke down, the buses were overloaded and stuck in traffic and no one went anywhere. The floodwaters found much of the population very much still in harm's way — the residents of rest homes, the inmates of prisons, the patients in hospitals still in their rooms, cells and wards. What a cock-up it was. The world watched riveted as a scene reminiscent of sub-Saharan Africa unfolded on telly — and we were asked to believe it was in America. The crowds huddled in the Superdome, shocked and awed stragglers trudged along deserted motorway overpasses, armed National Guardsmen patrolled against looters, and corpses rotted in the rubble.

T he picturesque tourist part of the city, the French Quarter, seemed surprisingly unscathed when we rolled in. We checked into a gorgeous hotel and discovered we could catch a jazz band in a club on Bourbon Street or dine in a quaint Basin Street eatery as though nothing had happened. It was easier to get into the clubs or book a table at a restaurant than before Katrina, as far fewer people had been visiting New Orleans since pictures of the hurricane damage went right around the world.

Before we left New Zealand, Roger, who had connections with the New York fire department, had managed to jack up digs for us in fire stations right across America. In New Orleans one of the firemen, Wayne Collongues, kindly offered to give up his day off and take us on a tour of the city the day after we arrived. So off we went.

The university suburbs were still full of Ivy League wannabes — young, white, swotting hard and getting on with their affluent after-hours activities as though nothing had happened. But as we got away from their comfy quarter and into the middle suburbs, we began to see signs of the devastation in the form of 'bath rings' a metre to two metres up the walls of houses. While it had surged higher, this is where the water level had settled for a period of three weeks.

A musty smell persisted and there were signs that things were only just starting out on the road to recovery — piles of garbage and building materials everywhere, trailers providing temporary accommodation for residents who had started on the heartbreaking business of rebuilding. Wayne showed us the fire chief's house, which had mouldered under a metre and a half of water for three weeks. Twenty-five of the city's fire stations had been destroyed, he said. His station's own appliances had escaped destruction because someone had had the foresight to evacuate them to higher ground.

That was nothing. The further out we got, into the poorer areas where tourists are forbidden to go, the higher the bath ring, the greater the destruction and the less likely it looked that things would ever be reconstructed. Wayne told us he'd been shot at while helping in the search and rescue effort in the flood's aftermath.

The lowest-lying part of pre-Katrina New Orleans now resembled nothing more than a landfill. We began seeing some pretty surreal sights: flash yachts stacked up on roadways where they'd been washed from distant marinas, some of them sporting wistful 'for sale' signs. Piles of cars, including stretch limousines, strewing the high-water mark. There was even a pile of motorbikes but, just as we began to fear the worst, we saw that they were all Hondas.

A fishing trawler sat in someone's back yard, hundreds of metres from the nearest permanent waterway. Houses that had been floated off their foundations rested against trees or other houses. Other homes had been completely smashed. Trees that had been ripped out of the ground lay dumped in heaps.

One thing was conspicuous by its absence in the worst-hit areas — the people. There was simply no one around, apart from bands of young Americans in matching T-shirts poking about in the rubble here and there, trying to clean up and rescue household items. They were religious youth groups here to do good deeds.

Many of the wrecked houses still bore the spray-painted symbols the searchers used to indicate when they were searched and how many bodies were found. Wayne interpreted for us. 'Searched on 9 September. No bodies.' 'Three cats. Unoccupied.' 'Searched 16 September. One body.' And nailed to the latter house — a simple, timber structure, bent in half by the upward pressure of the floodwaters — there was a wreath of red roses.

The scale of the devastation took our breath away but Wayne pointed out that it was so much better now than it had been just before Christmas. We were seeing the city after a massive clean-up operation.

Before Katrina rampaged ashore, there was real, grinding poverty in the danker, swampier parts of New Orleans such as District 9 — known locally just as 'the District' — and, naturally enough, plenty of crime perpetrated by the desperadoes who lived there, much of it against the property of the rich.

As we had seen for ourselves, the floods hit the lowest-lying areas hardest and since those areas were the poorest, it was the down-at-heel who suffered most.

By the time the storm had passed on, spending its fury in

the American interior, and once the floodwaters had finally receded, leaving much of the city smashed and covered in silt on the shores of the now toxic Lake Pontchartrain, 75 per cent of the population of New Orleans had been displaced. Many of these people will never return. Most of them were the poor.

It was hard to find many of the better-off citizens of the Big Easy who thought Katrina was a bad thing, apart from the temporary glitch it caused in their business fortunes. It was the judgment of the Lord, we heard from more than one source, sipping their mint juleps in the shade of well-appointed parlours in the lovely, leafy North District. Katrina was a scourge sent by Him against the sinners.

These views, of course, were expressed by white folks and it just so happened that most of those on the receiving end were black. Seventy per cent of the population of New Orleans was African American. Many of these people had jobs in the tourism industry. They'd surge into the French Quarter in the morning, spend the day pouring the drinks, tinkling the ivories, tooting the horns and singing the blues that the tourists expected, then head home again in the evening as the white citizens of the richer districts of New Orleans eyed them suspiciously through their window shades. While the American people are far too polite to say out loud that Katrina was a judicious act of ethnic cleansing by the Almighty, that notion was there all right, as a subtext in their conversation.

Much of the controversy about the Katrina disaster focused on how slow the relief effort was to mobilise and, of course, this gave rise to accusations that the relief effort was lethargic because most of the victims of the storm and the flood were black. George Dubya Bush and the rest of his good-ole-boy administration, it was suggested, just didn't care about the stricken because of their race.

This was certainly the view of those on the ground. We spoke to several black workers — all in menial jobs — who expressed bitter resentment at the disparity between blacks and whites in New Orleans. 'Us poor people are left to sit atop the piles of Katrina garbage,' one young black man told us, gesturing at the high life persisting in the French Quarter, 'and the gentry carry on as though nothing's happened.'

It has to be admitted that we were there at a pretty fraught time. The mayoral elections were on and one well-regarded African American candidate had played the race card in the course of his campaign, attempting to tap into the fury of the black population. He'd announced that he would like to see New Orleans rebuilt as a black city. But it's not as though the disaster created the racial division in New Orleans. Whatever veneer of complacency about race relations there is in America, it was warped and lifted by the floodwaters.

One day our resident bus nut Jo took one of the few trams that had survived the flood to the end of the line. It wasn't a very long line now, as Katrina had truncated the track. All the way there and back she quizzed the motorman, an elderly African American, about his city, the storm, his family and grandchildren.

'Where you from?' he asked her.

'New Zealand,' she replied.

He nodded.

'I knew it must be something like that. White folk don't

talk to black folk round here.'

He must have been right on that because at journey's end Jo got a big hug as she alighted — surely not the standard after-sales service he was accustomed to providing to his passengers.

Oh, America.

RIDING THE DRAGON

Most bikers contemplating a road trip of America will pencil in a date with the Dragon.

The Tail of the Dragon, working 318 corners into a stretch of North Carolina road only 18 km long, is an iconic piece of American motorcycling folklore. People trailer their bikes from all over the continent, from Mexico to Canada, book themselves into the Deal's Gap motel or campground and then race back and forth through the Dragon until they're satiated or come to grief, whichever comes first.

Our experience with it was a little different to this norm. We arrived at Townsend, Tennessee, in the evening and camped out on Smokey Mountain, fizzing with anticipation. We set out the next day with no ambitions of breaking the record for the transit of the Dragon. We were on touring bikes, and touring bikes loaded down with enough gear to see us through a four-month continental expedition ride at that, so we weren't at peak aerodynamic or handling performance.

Still, it's hard not to experience a surge of adrenaline once you hit the first curves, if only because you get overtaken by highway heroes going hell for leather, more often than not on blind bends. Better all round if you enter into the spirit of the occasion, lean forward, tighten your grip and twist the throttle.

As far from racing trim as our bikes may have been, Gareth still managed to come round a bend to be confronted with some American plonker and his wife riding two-up on their Harley hauling a trailer in what must have been second gear. We now know how good the brakes on the GS are — pretty damn good.

To ride, the Tail of the Dragon is not altogether different from a Sunday morning sprint up the Rimutakas to the north of Wellington, only much flatter from start to finish. What it lacks in gradient, however, it more than makes up for in the character of its curves. Many of these challenge you in three dimensions — you're taking a hard left-hander, say, when you're confronted with a gnarly little gut-swooping dip that's thrown in for good measure. It makes for a few tummy flutters as you hurl yourself through the sinuous, sculpted switchback but, like most American roads, the surface is beautiful and the camber and pitch calculated to the last degree.

The most sobering moment on our traverse came on corner 312 of the 318. The front bike had just leaned into a nice, tight right-hander when what should appear, coming in the other direction and mostly on our side of the road, but one of those huge articulated truck-and-trailer units. It was a solid and timely reminder of a potentially fatal truth — the Tail of the Dragon is not an official racetrack or some biker's fun park. It's a two-way public highway and everything on two wheels has to share it with vehicles rolling on anything up to 18.

We arrived, tired and exhilarated, at the Dragon's end, where stands the Tree of Shame — a tree bedecked with motorcycle parts from all those machines that didn't make it unscathed. As the boys lined up their bikes for the compulsory photo shoot to commemorate a job well done, arrogantly upright afore the strung-up chassis parts of those that had failed, the slope of the terrain scored a victory and their machines performed a domino-style collapse, drawing delighted applause from onlookers — Jo included — and red cheeks for themselves.

Jo missed the photo shoot, as she got talking to a huge, wildly bearded Texan welder named Bubba, whose eyes peered out from the tangle of his face fungus like a steer from a matagouri thicket. He was about to do the Dragon on his Harley.

Our experience with the truck, coming as it did toward the end of the traverse, somewhat tempered the urge to turn around and race back through, to see every corner from the opposite direction and shave a smidgeon off the trip time. So rather than try our luck again we moved on to Kickstand Lodge, a campground established, as its name suggests, for biker slayers of the Dragon. We spent a fabulous evening with the proprietors, Fred and Mo, and other guests, playing a fiercely competitive game of horseshoes and talking the experience through over a beautiful home-cooked meal. The road got more bendy, the dips sharper, the ride faster and the trucks bigger every time we told the tale of the Tail.

That night there was a spectacular thunderstorm, with lightning so bright and frequent you could sit in your tent reading by it. The rain turned the little stream that runs through the campground into a raging torrent but our trusty Fairydown tents kept us dry as dust.

COWBOYS AND INDIANS

It came as a bit of a shock to learn that Davy Crockett wasn't born on a mountaintop in Tennessee.

Gareth and Jo both grew up idolising the legendary 'king of the wild frontier'. Maybe it had something to do with the great frontiersman's motto, 'Be always sure you are right, then go ahead.' Whatever it was, as a kid Gareth got about in a coon-skin hat and a fringed buckskin suit — not unlike the sort you see Harley riders wearing today — and quickly wore out his 78 rpm record of *The Ballad of Davy Crockett*, with its dubious claim of Crockett's lofty birthplace. Meanwhile, unbeknown to Gareth, the young Jo was humming the same tune, stalking the wilds of Queen's Park, Invercargill, tomahawk in hand, looking for bears to slay.

When we were putting our itinerary together, it was clear that a visit to the Alamo, which Crockett died defending, was going to fit in nicely. And when we Googled him, we found that the site of Crockett's birth lay along the route as well.

It was in visiting the latter that we discovered the low-altitude truth about his birthplace. The site has been incorporated into a park at a little place called Limestone in Greene County, right up in the top right-hand corner of Tennessee. We found Davy Crockett Road and then the park itself, with a museum and a replica cabin on the spot where Crockett was born set amid a pleasant, grassy meadow at the confluence of the Nolichucky River and Limestone Creek. The water had been made muddy brown by heavy rain among the mountaintops upon which Davy Crockett was not born.

Upon arrival, Jo amazed us as usual by pulling a possum-skin Davy Crockett hat for each of us out of the cornucopia she calls a pannier. We donned these then set off a-whoopin' and a-hollerin' through the long grass, reliving childhood memories, before we sobered up enough to have a look around the museum.

The little cabin that stands where Davy was born is not the original — 220 years is a long time in the life of the softwood logs it was made out of — but the weathered monument marking the spot is one of the original foundations, suitably engraved by Crockett's grandson. We took photographs and wondered what it must have been like living in that little one-room shack with the snow piling up outside, just mum, dad and nine kids in a space where you couldn't swing a coon-skin hat.

Our own Davy — Wallace — told Gareth that he really should have loaded the song *Woody Woodpecker Meets Davy*

Crockett onto his iPod. Gareth had no idea what he was talking about.

'Course you do,' said Dave. 'Remember story time on the radio on Sunday mornings? They were always playing it.'

And he proceeded to sing it for us, dancing around and performing as good an imitation of the Woody Woodpecker laugh as it lies within the power of a Tauranga cocky to do. He had us in stitches.

Crockett may not have been born on a mountaintop but our research revealed that he scaled a few in his time. It turns out there was even more to the man than we had known or suspected. He was born in 1786, the fifth of his parents' children. Life in Greene County was pretty close to nature, as the little cabin brought home to us. But whether there's any truth to the rumour — which Crockett himself perpetuated — that he killed a bear when he was only three years old is anyone's guess.

After a dispute at school led to a row with his dad, who took a 'spare the rod, spoil the child' approach to discipline, the teenage Davy ran away from home and spent a few years wandering the wilds of Tennessee, hunting, shooting, fishing, tracking, trapping and generally living the red-blooded pioneer woodsman's life. His family had bought a pub in the meantime and when one day the king of the wild frontier wandered in to whet his whistle, one of his sisters recognised the tall, lean stranger in the buckskin duds and coon-skin hat. The prodigal son had returned and was welcomed back into the arms of his family, even by his dad — who presumably saw he might get his own hide tanned if he didn't.

When war broke out against the Creek Indians in 1813, Crockett joined up with the Tennessee Volunteer Mounted Riflemen and fought under the formidable General Andrew Jackson, known as Old Hickory and destined to become the seventh president of the United States. Crockett distinguished himself in the battle of Horseshoe Bend in Alabama, where Jackson led a mixture of militia and half the Creek nation against the other half.

After the war was over, Crockett spent a few more years hunting, shooting, fishing, trapping, et cetera, until he was elected to the United States House of Representatives in 1826. He was returned in 1828 and late in that two-year term he found himself leading the opposition to a bill being bulldozed through Congress by the president, none other than his old commander Andrew Jackson. Jackson had been elected on the strength of his prowess at kicking Indian butt and his new law was intended to give him the power and the wherewithal to negotiate treaties to relocate all Indians from the land east of the Mississippi River into the west, thus freeing up all that prime eastern real estate for white settlement.

Crockett was as much an underdog in his unpopular stance sticking up for the Indian as he was later in life at the Alamo. He lost his seat on the strength of it. Jackson prevailed. His Indian Removal Act was passed in 1830 and he wasted little time in entering negotiations to ethnically cleanse the east. Jackson's track record didn't bode too well for the prospects of good faith — his first act after whipping the Creeks was to hammer out a treaty with the vanquished chiefs, whereby they ceded to him most of what later became Alabama —

never mind that the other half of the Creek nation, his allies in the Battle of Horseshoe Bend, were bitterly opposed. Injuns, so far as Jackson was concerned, was Injuns.

***

Most people know Chattanooga from the 1941 Glenn Miller Big Band hit *Chattanooga Choo Choo*. We rolled into the city the song made famous on a Friday, still buzzing after the previous day's ride on The Dragon.

Chattanooga's a fairly unprepossessing place, as you'd expect of an industrial town. For a while in the 1930s it was known as 'the dynamo of Dixie' for the scale of its industry. But it fell on hard times and was declared America's dirtiest city in the 1960s, with decades of noxious emissions trapped over the plain it occupies by the aptly named Great Smoky Mountains. It's had a bit of a spruce-up since then and now boasts some unusual attractions.

Predictably, there's a fair bit of activity centred around the Choo Choo. Jo spent the best part of an hour swapping tales with the retired navy man who was now its driver and conductor. At the end of their deliberations, the rest of us were still none the wiser as to whether driving a trolley bus around Wellington was more challenging than handling the old steam train.

The train pulls into a large, kitschy precinct that has been constructed in the vicinity of the former Chattanooga Terminal Station, restored since passenger rail was withdrawn from the city in 1970. Parked up here is one of the original trains that plied the southern railroads in the days the little Choo Choo ditty was penned. You can stay at the

Choo Choo Holiday Inn if you wish, in half a restored Choo Choo sleeper car, or you can dine in a genuine Choo Choo dining car.

If that doesn't grab you, there are other attractions. The city's railway connections meant that when the American National Model Railroad Association was looking for a new headquarters, Chattanooga was a natural choice. And there's always the International Towing and Recovery Hall of Fame and Museum — we kid you not — because Chattanooga, bless it, is known as the place that gave the world tow trucks and towies.

Just about equally ignominious is Chattanooga's significance in the history of relations between white and native Americans.

The land that Chattanooga occupies was continuously occupied by Indians from around AD 900, although various tribal groups came and went. By the time the white settlers started exerting pressure on the inhabitants, it was the great Cherokee tribe that was resident.

Like the Creeks, the Cherokee were one of the so-called 'civilised tribes' that had accommodated and even embraced the encroachment of white settlers. In fact, the Cherokee were the most 'civilised' of the lot. Most were Christians, and a linguistically inclined tribe member called Sequoyah had developed a written syllabic script for the Cherokee language. The Cherokee Nation had a written constitution and was governed by a democratically elected assembly.

It was Thomas Jefferson, the third president of the United States, who first had the bright idea of shifting Indians from the eastern states, where there were plenty of them, to the west, where there were none, to form a buffer between the American settlements in the east and the menacing presence of the English and the Spanish in the west. What's more, since 1802 there had been steady pressure on the federal government to remove the pesky Indians who stood in the way of the decent, God-fearing white folk who were trying to push inland from the main settlements on the eastern seaboard. In that year, the sprawling state of Georgia had ceded a huge tranche of territory — these days we call it Mississippi and Alabama — to the government in return for a promise to do just that.

Trouble was, the Indians didn't want to go. The Creeks, as we've already mentioned, went to war over it. The Cherokee set up their own apparatus of government in 1820 and made it clear that they meant to stay right where they were and get on with it. In 1825 they founded a capital at New Echota, close to the town of Calhoun in present-day Georgia, and in 1827 declared themselves independent from the rest of the United States.

Andrew Jackson was elected president in 1828 on a promise not just to talk the talk of shifting the Indians but to have them walk the walk. As we know now, it was a walk to virtual oblivion — from the lush Appalachians to the arid deserts west of the Mississippi. With providential good timing, as it must have seemed to Jackson, gold was discovered in Georgia, sparking a gold rush and a spike in demand for land. There was gold in them thar hills — so it was darn inconvenient that there was Injuns too. The Indian Removal Act passed Congress in 1830 with Crockett almost a lone voice in opposition.

The hapless Choctaw Indians were the first to be strong-armed into signing a removal treaty and shipped out. About 12,500 were sent west in 1831 and between 2000 and 4000 died on the way, most of cholera. A treaty was signed with the Seminoles in 1832, although it took a decade and a bit of a stoush to actually shift them. Nearly 20,000 Creeks were next, shown the state door between 1834 and 1837, with 3500 dying along the way.

After a bit of wrangling over the status of the Cherokee Nation in the Supreme Court, Jackson moved in to get the tribe to sign its own eviction warrant in 1835. He managed to assemble a crowd of prominent Cherokee at New Echota and got 20 of them to sign the Treaty of Echota, under which the Cherokee forfeited their lands east of the Mississippi in exchange for land to the west of the great river and $5 million in cash. None of the Cherokee signatories had any authority to execute the treaty — none was an elected representative of the Cherokee National Assembly — but that didn't matter to Jackson. More than 15,000 Cherokee signed a petition in protest but Jackson managed to get the treaty ratified by the Senate in May 1836, albeit by a margin of a single vote.

The government then moved to put the treaty into effect, sending troops to round 'em up and move 'em out. About 17,000 were crowded into stockaded camps ready for removal. Disease in the camps was rife, and the hardships the people faced on the 1900 km trek west were extreme. It had been envisaged that they would travel by the so-called Water Route, using boats on the rivers and lakes, but the first contingents to set out found the rivers too low to navigate. They were forced to resort to travel on foot or by wagon.

They dropped like flies.

By the time 21,500 men, women and children of the displaced Cherokee had made it to Indian territory — modern-day Oklahoma — thousands had died. Some estimate the toll to have been 2000. Others reckon it could have been as high as 8000. Little wonder that the route and the calamity that befell them on it are known to the Cherokee as 'the Trail of Tears'.

In all, 100,000 Indians were shifted from the South under the Indian Removal Act. It was the turn of the Chickasaws in 1837 and the last of the Seminoles were shifted out in 1842. The rosiest estimate of the fatal impact of the policy is 7500 dead, the bleakest 16,000, to say nothing of the fact that those who survived were forced to abandon their ancestral lands and the greater part of their worldly possessions. Some even watched as white looters moved in to ransack the houses they had been forced to vacate at gunpoint.

One admirable thing about Americans is that they don't flinch from the ugly bits in their own history, or at least not at an official level. There are monuments and national parks dedicated to all manner of dodgy, dubious and outright deplorable incidents in their past, and the tragic ethnic cleansing of the South is no exception.

We spent quite a few days riding down one of the old trails of the Choctaw — the Natchez Trace trail, that runs for 715 km from Nashville, Tennessee, down to Natchez, Mississippi, crossing the lands of the Choctaw and Chickasaw. Not only is it one of the most lush and beautiful parkways in the United States, with deer frequently daring us to lose control of our bikes, but it's rich in Indian history, with ceremonial mounds forming the majority of the historical sites. The ghost of Davy Crockett stalks it and even that cruel old dog General Jackson, who had marched his army down this way to fight the Battle of New Orleans against the British before he turned his hand to Indian cleansing, is commemorated by the occasional memorial along the way. As we stood on our hotel balcony at Natchez looking west into the sunset over the Mississippi River and the flatlands of Louisiana on the other side, we wondered what it must have been like for those Indians being forced ever west for the convenience of the European settlers.

In 1987, Congress decreed the Trail of Tears a national historic trail, stretching 3540 km through nine states. It starts on the banks of the Tennessee River in Chattanooga at a place called Ross's Landing, named for John Ross, a Cherokee leader in the 1830s who organised resistance to the forceful removal and who lost his wife in the forced march.

Given the huge historical significance of the Trail of Tears, we visited Ross's Landing. Frankly it's a bit disappointing — two large bridges straddle the banks at the spot where the internment camp or 'emigration depot' was sited. But it still seemed unreal, when we looked down from the bridge to the landing, that on this spot the curtain was brutally closed on a culture that had done no wrong. And this just 50 years after the country was formed on the premise 'that all men are created equal, and that they are endowed by their Creator with certain unalienable rights, among these the right to life, liberty and the pursuit of happiness'. It brings home just how different the practice of politics often is to the fine, rhetorical principles upon which it is founded.

And what of Davy? In 1835, Crockett offered his services to the people of Tennessee as their congressman for the last time. 'I told the people of my district that I would serve them as faithfully as I had done,' he wrote in his memoirs. 'But if not, you may all go to hell and I will go to Texas.' Sure enough, they voted for the Indians to be removed, he missed out on Congress and, man of his word that he was, he went to Texas.

Texas had been opened up by Spanish explorers and was then a part of Mexico, although it was settled in the late 18th century as a kind of joint venture between Americans and Mexicans, who called themselves Texians and Tejans respectively. With plenty of fast talking by the Texians, this arrangement survived the Mexican war of independence from Spain and several changes of regime in Mexico itself, including the assumption of power in 1833 by the Mexican war hero, strongman, president and then dictator, Antonio de Padua María Severino López de Santa Anna y Pérez de Lebrón, cryptically known as Santa Anna and more generally in his own day as 'sir'.

It wasn't without friction, however. Then, as now, Texas was having problems with illegal immigrants, although it's one of those picturesque quirks of history that in those days it was a matter of too many Americans sneaking in, rather than Mexicans. And back then, the Texians chafed under

Left: *So tell me, is New Zealand a windy place?*

Below: *Coffee and noodles . . . our typical roadside fare.*

Above: *Once were slave dwellings on the plantation . . .*

Above: *A cancer patient wheels her drip outide so she can puff on a cigarette.*

Below: *. . . and the Master's house.*

Above: *Katrina-fied limo, New Orleans.*

Below: *Fats Domino's house in District 9, New Orleans.*

Above: *Ready for the next Hurricane Katrina — Louisiana.*

Below: *Hurricane Rita ripped the housing from here — Texas.*

Above: *Happy and innocent kids — Mexico.*

Right: *Roger fitting right in with the Mexican Indian locals.*

Below: *Winding down into Copper Canyon, Mexico.*

Above: *Hot springs in the Chihuahua desert? Crazy.*

Below: *Ancient Indian village remains — New Mexico.*

Above: *Indian reservation. Nice housing, eh?*

Below: *How? — Roger pow-wows in Navajo country, Arizona.*

Above: *Four riders, four states all at once — at the Four Corners monument, Arizona, Colorado, New Mexico and Utah!*

Below: *Jo being divisive — Zion National Park, Utah.*

restrictions imposed on their economic activities — notably slavery — by the Mexican government.

Tensions escalated into armed conflict in 1835 and the Texians sought to establish an army to fight for the state's independence. To attract soldiers they offered plots of land in return for military service. Perhaps it was the prospect of his own little slice of Texas that lured Davy Crockett or perhaps it was adventure that drew him at the age of 49 to enlist to fight against the Mexicans.

***

Sunday 21 May was a long day for us, the longest on the trip so far, 486 km down the Interstate through Texas from Orange to San Antonio. We passed through Houston, sticking strictly to the Interstate, as we had a date to keep further south. Houston reminded us that we were very much in JR Ewing country (although his hometown, Dallas, is a little further north). First the skyscrapers loomed large on the desert horizon, then as we approached the city the roading system emerged in all its complexity. We seemed to whizz through a maze of criss-crossing expressways, going over some and plunging under others, feeling quite dizzy as we were finally spat back out into the desert on the other side of town. Auckland's Spaghetti Junction has a long way to go before it can bewilder the motorist the way Houston can. We booked into our hotel, within musket range of the site of the Alamo in downtown San Antonio.

This old Spanish mission building is the most visited tourist attraction in Texas and an emblem of American heroism, as they see it, for the cause of liberty. It's also the final resting place of Davy Crockett. Nowadays it's a museum, and museums are things the Americans do very well, with re-enactments throughout the day of scenes from the battles and other activities the Alamo site has witnessed. Inside the walled compound, the chapel still stands and the museum displays Davy's buckskin vest and a couple of flintlock rifles from the battle. Also still holding up is the Palisade, a section of the fort defended by Crockett and co.

***

By the end of February 1836, El Presidente, Generalissimo and self-proclaimed Boss of the World Santa Anna and his army were nearing San Antonio, determined to snuff out the gringo secessionist movement. His force numbered upward of 1500. Opposing him in the Alamo were 150-odd Americans.

Their leader, William Travis, had sent out a call for reinforcements but it was ignored by the commander of the disorganised Texas Army. However, a bunch of infantrymen decided to answer the call on their own initiative and reinforcements duly arrived, all 30 of them. They managed to sneak through the Mexican army, which was probably on the lookout for a battalion-sized relief party, and entered the Alamo.

It was a one-way trip. Travis assembled his men shortly before the fighting began in earnest and told them they had three choices. First, to make a single, desperate sortie in the hope they could take a few Mexicans with them. Second, to surrender and almost certainly be massacred. (Santa Anna had a bit of a rep in this regard. He had massacred the rebel garrison of Zacatecas a few years previously and rewarded his troops with a 48-hour licence to rape and pillage the civilian population. He also gave no quarter to the defenders of the fort at Goliad.)

The third option was to defend the Alamo to the last man, delaying Santa Anna's advance and giving the ragtag Texan army time to get its shit together. To a man, they chose the third.

The story of the gallant 13-day defence has been told many times. It ended the only way it possibly could, with the garrison overwhelmed. Six defenders are said to have survived the fighting, only to be summarily put to the sword on Santa Anna's orders. Crockett is supposed to have been among them. The bodies of the entire garrison were cremated, apart from one who was related to one of the Mexican soldiers and was buried, as a Catholic gesture of respect.

It's a story that has everything for Americans — the goodies, underdogs and heroes, fighting selflessly for freedom against a brutal dictator. It's the blueprint for every war the United States has subsequently entered, though few have turned out the way Hollywood would prefer it.

By the time Santa Anna locked horns with the Texan Army at San Jacinto on 26 April it had become a formidable outfit, fired up by their leader, Sam Houston, who urged them to 'Remember the Goliad! Remember the Alamo!' The Mexicans were defeated and Texas won its independence, becoming a republic. Santa Anna had another go at restoring the Lone Star state to Mexican rule in 1842 but this merely convinced the Texans to join the United States, as its 28th state, in 1845.

In Mexico we were privileged to see American Indians living a relatively traditional lifestyle — something that is no longer possible in the United States. The Tarahumara Indians were once widely dispersed across Chihuahua, the northwestern part of Mexico, but the Spanish conquistadors drove them back into the Copper Canyon, high in the Sierra Madre Occidentale. When minerals were found there in the 20th century and mining began they retreated further still.

The cool thing about the Tarahumara is that they have all but isolated themselves from the modern world. The women dress in long, colourful cotton dresses while the men get about in loincloths and tyre-soled sandals. Apparently they live in caves in the winter and cabins in the summer and spend most of their time tending their gardens of corn and beans and their herds of cattle, goats and the odd sheep. They're remarkable-looking people, small of stature, their skin tanned and lined like old leather, with very dark eyes. Their own name for themselves is *raramuri*, which loosely translates as 'foot throwers'. Foot-throwing is running, which the Tarahumara do pretty well — centuries of living in the rugged Sierra Madre with long distances between settlements turned them into a nation of ultra-marathon runners. They hold foot-throwing competitions, in which the competitors will run more than 150 km through the desert, kicking little wooden balls ahead of them all the way — Arthur Lydiard eat your heart out.

Visiting the Tarahumara in their lost world was a real culture shock after the United States, where there are only remnants of native American culture to be seen. On our way across the New Mexico desert we visited the Bandelier

Pueblo Indian ruins, which date back to the very early days of permanent Indian settlement, about four thousand years ago. The chalky cliffs of the canyon at Bandelier are honeycombed with the caves in which the Pueblo Indians lived for about five hundred years, before a sudden change in the climate and a couple decades of drought drove them south in search of water and arable land. We found similar ruins in the dusty Mesa Verde in Colorado.

We had seen other evidence of Indian habitation earlier on the ride, from Jamestown, Virginia, where a Powhatan Indian settlement is commemorated in a museum, to the sites all through the Appalachians and along the Natchez Trace trail. Certainly the Trail of Tears was the beginning of the end of the great story of native American culture. The wars with the Indians in the early days of European settlement and the orderly genocide carried out under the Indian Removal Act reached their logical conclusion at Wounded Knee, South Dakota, where 150 Lakota Indians were massacred by troops in 1890. It was an atrocity but really only one of a series of atrocities over the history of European settlement of America. It was a low point in the shared history of the races but we're talking a pothole in the floor of a canyon.

Sadly, the legacy of this chequered past of ethnic cleansing is still there for all to see. Travelling north from Cortez in Colorado, we visited 'the Big Rez', the vast reservation occupied by the Navajo Nation, straddling the corners of four states, Colorado, Arizona, New Mexico and Utah. The standard of housing is shocking, with most families living in little concrete-block houses in the searing desert heat or in that ubiquitous low-budget American accommodation option, the trailer, which in these locations is like an oven, so they are parked in the shade of the few trees on offer. The once-proud Navajo people make their money these days selling trinkets to passing tourists or parting them from their cash in Navajo casinos. Talk about depressing — the Australians and their treatment of Aborigines have good competition in the way the Americans have dealt to their Indian population.

Yippee-yi-yay.

NO, AFTER YOU

One thing we noticed right away about biking in the United States — the home of the automobile — is that motorist behaviour is infinitely more courteous than it is back home. While the traffic tends to move a lot faster than is permitted in New Zealand — it's not unusual when travelling at 100 km/h to be passed by 18-wheeler lorries doing 125 km/h — there's a notable lack of aggression in everything they do.

Then again, we've noticed the same thing in most of the countries we've travelled in.

The thing that America has in common with Germany, say, or Bulgaria and that sets it apart from New Zealand is that there is far less regulation of driver behaviour. Drivers are expected to be responsible for their own actions and dependent upon the courtesy of others. Rather than relying on a rule to tell them how to behave, they are guided by the principle of cooperation.

It's a clever discretion of the rule-makers. Regulatory latitude gives rise to a 'do as you would be done by' ethos. For example, in the United States there are a lot more four-way intersections without traffic lights. They have four stop signs instead. The convention is first-come, first-served — the vehicle that's first to arrive at its stop sign is given the right of way, the vehicle that arrives second at its sign goes next and so on. It's a sort of enforced courtesy. The system simply cannot function if the code of behaviour isn't followed. Drivers have no choice but to make decisions themselves and, surprise, surprise, they rise to the challenge. It turns out there's no need for a rule for every situation. People work it out among themselves. Needless to say, it warmed the cockles of Gareth's anarcho-capitalist heart to see spontaneous coordination of this nature in action.

Better yet, courtesy — like king-of-the-road aggression — is infectious and prevails in every situation drivers encounter. For example, if our lead bike came out of a byway onto a highway where the traffic density didn't allow room for the second bike to follow immediately, the traffic would stop and wave the next bike through. No one leans on their horn, delivers a one-finger salute or tailgates you for the next hundred kilometres to get their point across. Coming from New Zealand, it all took a little getting used to. If you approached the side of a busy highway on foot the traffic would come to a complete stop, the drivers genially signalling you to cross. That *certainly* took some getting used to!

There were plenty of other examples of how lightly the hand of regulation sits — and how much faith the regulator has in the capacity of individuals to make intelligent choices for themselves. If you're at a red light but you can turn to the right (it would be to the left in New Zealand) without danger, you can go ahead and do it. On the open road a speed limit can be exceeded by up to 15 kmh without placing you at risk of receiving a ticket. So if the speed limit is 110 kmh you can happily travel at 125 kmh.

This convention had us stumped until, sick of being passed while riding piously at the limit, Jo decided to interrogate a radar-gunning cop about how the system worked. Our Kiwi paranoia naturally had us thinking every mile per hour over the limit would see us stung a tidy sum in fines.

'Well, little lady,' CHiPs responded, 'over here we like to see you get from A to B as quickly as possible. So as long as the traffic is orderly we don't worry too much about the speed. Way we figure it, highways are supposed to be of service to the travelling public. I'm just after the maniacs.'

Jo congratulated him on the sanity of this approach to law enforcement and made to leave.

'Hey!' he called after her. 'Make sure you keep up with the traffic. You'll be safe that way.'

The only time Jo did get pulled up was in Montana, by a cop who saw rain a-coming and was worried that she didn't have her wet gear on.

'You'll get five minutes down the road,' he told her, 'then them clouds are going to open right up. You'll be soaked through.'

He finished by asking if she'd like some maps of the area! Does this seem a long way from cop behaviour in New Zealand?

Motorcyclists in many states of America are free to choose

whether or not to wear helmets. We wore ours most of the time but it was great having the right to shed them every now and then at our discretion and feel the wind in our hair. Remember when it was like that in New Zealand? That was before we sank into a swill of smothering maternalistic supervision.

Stifling over-regulation such as the laws that prevail in New Zealand creates automatons; morons who need rules and regulations to determine their behaviour for them. People lose the skills that the freedom to make decisions fosters. Sure, lower speeds lower the road toll — but so would banning driving altogether.

This is not to say the power of the state in America is not there, hovering in the background. Their road code has fewer rules but it also has far higher fines — and there is also the fear of being sued if you screw up. Responsibility is very much on individuals — the law treats them almost as though they're grown-ups.

THE MELTING POT

No one can say we're afraid of going to extremes. We began our tour of America at the eastern extremity of the North American landmass and there were a couple of compelling reasons to work a visit to the westernmost point into the itinerary too.

The Bahamas is where Christopher Columbus first sighted the New World and commenced the European history of America. The western tip of Cape Prince of Wales, Alaska, is not only the most westerly point of the American mainland, it's also the point from which the original human inhabitants of the continent began their colonisation. There was a pleasing symmetry to the notion of book-ending our tour with these sites of first contact.

So one Friday in early July we boarded our chartered Piper Navajo and set out from Fairbanks for the little town of Nome, out on the Alaskan coast. Our pilot, Matt

Anderson, came highly recommended by some fellow Kiwis who had been following our trip on the web. Matt, they said, had excellent aerobatic skills. We just wanted confirmation he had mastered take-off, landing and level flight. Once we were satisfied on this score we were off, flying over what seemed to be most of the three million lakes of 8 hectares or more that this state of wetlands boasts and that together cover more than 20 per cent of the landmass.

The subsoil here is deep-frozen, with a permafrost anything from 2 km to 6 km thick, giving surface water in the summer nowhere to go but sideways. It sits about in lakes that carry on growing until they spill into rivers or the winter freeze comes around again. Meanwhile they support a flourishing flora and a range of browsing fauna such as moose and caribou.

The shadow of the plane sped along the tundra, following the twists and turns of that most famous of rivers, the Yukon, down to where it empties into the Bering Sea in Norton Sound. From here we skipped northwest over ice-bound beaches to the town of Nome, humming Andy Horton's song *North to Alaska* and indeed crossing over 'the old white mountain a little southeast of Nome' mentioned in the lyrics. After a quick fuel stop on the ground at Nome we pushed further north-west to Wales, essentially an Eskimo fishing camp huddled on a bleak beach.

The conventional theory on the origins of the indigenous peoples of the Americas — including the Eskimo and Inuit — is that they strolled across a land bridge that traversed the Bering Strait at a time when a good proportion of the world's seawater was frozen in the polar regions, during the latter years of the last ice age, about 12,000 years ago. They hunted musk ox, mammoth and polar bear along the way before finding their way down between two North American ice sheets into the more temperate climes of the land of freedom. Why? Given the later history of American immigration, it's likely they were fleeing persecution or competition for scarce resources in their homeland, supposed to have been in Central Asia or Siberia. Archaeological sites associated with these people — known as the Clovis culture — have been found the length and breadth of both Americas.

New evidence has emerged, though, as new evidence tends to do, to challenge this theory. Earlier sites yet have been found, and work on the language and genetics of indigenous Americans has suggested that the Home of the Brave was settled far earlier, perhaps as long ago as 40,000 years, and maybe by boat rather than on foot. It has been speculated that the same intrepid folk who set out across the Pacific to discover and settle its islands, becoming the Polynesians, also carried out a series of coast-hopping colonisation expeditions in a great circle from South Asia to Siberia and across the chain of the Aleutian Islands and down the Pacific coast of the Americas.

To honour the spirits of these first, intrepid migrants, Gareth had planned a little stunt — or, more correctly, a deed dumber than anything *Jackass* could contrive. Only by trying to recreate, albeit in reverse, the crossing from Siberia to Alaska, he reasoned, could he really gain a proper appreciation of the hardships those ancestors of the Eskimo and the North, Central and South American Indians faced.

A couple of days earlier we had paid a visit to the Fairbanks Wal-Mart where, for a little more than $11 (NZ$18), he bought a Waverider, a plastic one-man inflatable dinghy with three separate buoyancy chambers to ensure you stay afloat even if you strike adversity and the integrity of any one compartment is compromised. For a few dollars more, he added a pair of paddles made from laminated Alaskan spruce.

The weather on our arrival at Wales, the launching-pad for this attempt at a grand commemorative crossing of the Bering Strait, left a bit to be desired. We struggled against the wind to open the hatch of the aircraft to get ourselves and Gareth's seafaring gear out. And despite it being only 65.5 degrees north, just below the Arctic Circle and well south of the spot where we'd had a dip in the Beaufort Sea, where it was bitter. The sight of pack ice just to the north and the ice formed along the beach made this escapade far from enticing. Still, too late to chicken out now.

Dauntless, Gareth togged up in his Icebreaker undies and Gore-Tex overclothes and we set off for the beach. Even this hundred-metre walk posed its challenges. The village graveyard lies between the airstrip and the high-water mark and the wind here is grisly. We walked through the wooden crosses in the dunes, stopping to photograph a Honda trail bike lying among the crosses — presumably they buried the rider where he fell — down to the beach. Rampant coastal erosion means the mortal remains of ex-villagers don't get to rest in peace for very long. Human skulls and femurs and other bleached bits and pieces whose form was morbidly familiar littered the landscape. We had to pick our way gingerly through this debris of centuries of Eskimo habitation to get to the water, watching our step lest we deliver a swift and disrespectful kick to the skull of someone's dear departed.

Down by the water, with a leaden swell crashing onto the sand, Gareth stowed everything he'd need for the dash to Siberia — lifejacket, satellite phone, emergency bleeper, food rations and his passport — not! He had little more than a New Zealand flag aboard. The polar conditions shrivelled even his lunchbox to puny proportions. He handed a letter to Jo with instructions to deliver it to his mother if, as he put it, anything should happen to him.

The ceremonials complete, in a wind that bent the spine like a supple willow, he plonked his Waverider in the shallows, dumped his bag aboard (no, not Jo; she sagely stuck to the shore, preferring to record this momentous event on film) and pushed off on his epic reconstruction of those early migratory voyages.

He didn't get too far on his first attempt. The Waverider faced its first test at the very first line of breakers, overturning in a flurry of white water and even whiter shins, disgorging our intrepid adventurer into the Bering Strait.

Undeterred, he floundered ashore, emptied the water from his craft and prepared to mount a second attempt.

This time the Waverider mastered the first line of rollers and even the second, Gareth's spruce paddles flashing as he dug furiously at the sea, but it proved no equal to the towering walls of green and chill water of the third rank. It was a dejected sailor who trudged up the beach, frozen through and defeated, moments after the strait repelled him.

He called it quits, his objective — Siberia — nought but a fading dream. After all, his business is all about managing risk and respecting volatility, random noise and all those other technical terms that are used to describe events beyond our control. In the ferocious Bering Strait surf, no less than in the world of finance, should his experience indicate that reality threatens to overwhelm prognosis, he's prepared to change his plans to suit the situation. Scourge of the New Zealand Minister of Finance and the funds management industry he may be. Nanook of the North he is not.

Our short flight back to Nome was uneventful but our stay at this hub of the Eskimo region was anything but. The people were hugely hospitable. Jim West, who seems to own the town, was especially welcoming and organised for Dave to go fishing in the local stream. Within 30 minutes he returned with six fine humpies — the local pink salmon. As if that weren't enough, Jim's partner Veronica then cooked them up and served us all a magnificent lunch at the tables in the Bingo Hall on Front St, one of Jim's many establishments, with uninterrupted views across the Bering Strait.

Meanwhile, still frustrated at our failure so far to sight a musk ox despite all these miles ridden and flown across Alaska, we were picked up by Richard of Nome, a character if ever there was one. With all the ebullience of someone more at home on the Broadway stage than the furthest reaches of the American continent, Richard whisked us in his clapped-out van up into the hills where he'd passed a herd of musk ox just yesterday. We were excited.

After an hour of thump and bump across the tundra we had learned a lot about Richard but naff-all of the whereabouts of our elusive, aromatic, furry prey. Yes, he had been an understudy to Joel Grey in *Cabaret* —man, did he look and act that part — and he'd come to Alaska to escape the alcoholism that's part and parcel of life as a struggling theatrical aspirant. He started off selling fridges and freezers, of all things, to Eskimos — final proof to the locals that he could talk the legs off a chair — then he moved into radio and theatre and had spent the least 20 years entertaining all those who come to Nome.

Snatching opportunity from the jaws of defeat, Richard leapt from the van and literally started to skip the light fantastic across the tundra, inviting Jo to step along and be his partner for this botanical flit through the flora on the hillside. During the summer the tundra is a kaleidoscope of colour, many of the plants less than an inch high but coming in a dazzling variety of shapes and shades. With all the extravagant flourishes of David Bellamy, Richard was able to name and recite the natural history of every plant we skipped across — it was an impressive demonstration by this ex-fridge salesman and star of the New York stage. But in the end we returned to Nome, musk ox-less.

This is one of the harshest permanently inhabited parts of the world and apart from a few balmy weeks the locals see snow year-round — perhaps that's why Richard was so light-headed and overflowing with *joie de vivre* when we came across him. That people have lived here for centuries is a tribute to their tenacity and endurance and to the way human cultures adapt to the rigours of their particular environments.

Inevitably, the traditional way of life that has sustained them down the years is under threat. There's tension between the old and the new, as the advent of mining in the region has brought to the Eskimo both good changes (wages) and bad (liquor and drugs). But ranked against what their ancestors surmounted to survive in this godforsaken part of the world, the challenges presented by the encroachments of the modern world are trifling. There's every reason to believe the traditional Eskimo way of life will survive.

By the time Columbus misnamed the people he found in the Bahamas 'Indians', the descendants of those first Bering Strait pedestrians had spread from their beachhead somewhere near Wales, Alaska, to every part of North, Central and South America.

As we've noted, the Spanish were not necessarily the next colonists to arrive in America. The Vikings were established in Newfoundland and the Chinese may have preceded Columbus in the West Indies.

As we've also mentioned, the colonisation of America proceeded in several waves after the Spanish established a toehold at St Augustine, Florida, in 1565. The English were next, at Jamestown, South Carolina in 1607. Then a Dutch vessel established Fort Orange on the banks of the Hudson River in 1609 and set up a trading port on the island of Manhattan, which was purchased entire from the local Indian tribe for a handful of beads and a few pocket knives

— who says commercial property investment's a mug's game? A bunch of Swedes founded New Sweden in Delaware Bay in 1638 and in the 1670s disaffected Frenchmen from the colony at Quebec surveyed the Mississippi and founded Arcadia in present-day Louisiana (the word 'Cajun' is an English corruption of 'Arcadian').

America attracted these assorted nationalities during the colonial period of its history because it was a blank slate on which something new and better than the Old World could be sketched and built. And this was the pattern of the subsequent phase too. The arrival of an immigrant ship in an American port invariably notified the outbreak of some form of nastiness in another part of the world. Two million Irish arrived in the decade to 1854, a quarter of the country's population, fleeing the ravages of the potato famine of the 1840s. The failure of a revolution in Germany sent a wave of Germans across the Atlantic in the 1850s, many of them Jews. A large contingent of their Russian co-religionists followed in the late 1800s, refugees from the pogroms visited upon them in the wake of the assassination of Alexander II. Close to three million Italians emigrated from their overcrowded homeland between 1890 and 1910 and millions more followed throughout the 20th century.

The success of migrant communities in America gave rise to one of its most cherished myths, the American Dream. Anyone could get ahead provided they worked hard — just look at some of those who started out penniless and ended up in positions of wealth, status and power. John Davison Rockefeller and Teddy Roosevelt started out as the children of humble migrants and worked their way up to become, respectively, one of the richest men in the world and president of the United States. All it took, if you believe the hype, was elbow grease and a belief in the American Way.

A poem written by Emma Lazarus and inscribed on the base of the Statue of Liberty reads:

Give me your tired, your poor,
Your huddled masses yearning to breathe free,
The wretched refuse of your teeming shore.
Send these, the homeless, tempest-tost to me,
I lift my lamp beside the golden door!

The 20th century heralded no end to the supply of huddled masses yearning to breathe free and for the most part they were welcomed into American society. There were occasional lapses when the golden door was slammed shut. The most notorious of these was just prior to World War II when the *SS St Louis*, carrying more than 950 Jewish refugees from persecution in Nazi Germany, was refused permission to land her passengers in Florida. The United States was not alone. Several other countries, notably Cuba and Canada, refused to accept the *St Louis's* hapless complement, with the result that she returned to Europe. Those who couldn't be placed in other European countries fell back into the hands of the Nazis and were sent to the death camps. Even many of those who were landed in countries such as Belgium, France or the Netherlands fared no better, as these soon fell under German occupation and they were rounded up too. It was a pretty dismal chapter in the story of a pretty dismal century.

It has been noted that American immigration policy has tightened markedly since the 11 September 2001 terrorist attacks on American soil. Yet America still accepts more migrants as permanent residents than the rest of the world combined. Certainly everywhere we went we encountered people who were, to more or less a degree of obviousness, of immigrant stock. Americans with the swarthiness of Italians, if not the accent. Black African Americans and brown Polynesian Americans. People who looked Chinese, Japanese or South-East Asian but who spoke like Uncle Sam. And, everywhere we went, Hispanic Americans. The importance of Mexican migrants to the United States economy cannot be underestimated. One night in a bar in Pecos, Texas, which is famous for a penitentiary that holds mainly illegal Mexican migrants, we struck up a conversation with three Hispanic road workers. Pointing out the irony that the town's main business seem to be the confinement of Mexicans yet most of its labour force were immigrants, one of the boys commented that there was a right way to enter the United States and a wrong way.

'Oh? And what's the right way?' Gareth asked.

'When you don't get caught,' he replied dryly.

Funnily enough, these guys all supported the moves afoot to stem the flow of migrants. And that's the irony in the anti-migrant constituency — this is an economy still building itself on migrant labour, much of it illegal but nevertheless indispensable. Another man, an African, confided to us that he was an illegal immigrant, having flown into Mexico and then come across the border in the back of a truck. After being in the country for 10 years he married an American citizen and became legal.

The United States is a melting pot of multiculturalism, thanks to its relatively open-door policy toward migrants. Strange then that it is so concerned about immigration from its neighbour immediately to the south, Mexico. At Laredo, where we crossed from Texas to Mexico on a hot June afternoon, we saw hundreds of people lined up on a bridge to cross the Rio Grande from Mexico to work at their menial stateside day jobs in car assembly plants and other manufacturing concerns, most of which have lately shifted to Texas precisely so that they can get ready access to this steady stream of cheap labour. In the evening the flow was reversed as they were herded home again. Thousands of Mexicans hold down contract positions in America, and their numbers will grow if George Bush has his way. These are the lucky ones.

Laredo is a shabby town, with desperation hanging palpably in the air. Not only is it a centre of human traffic, it's also a major node in the flow of the cocaine that drifts from South and Central America north to disappear up the nostrils of Americans with nose-candy habits. Consequently, the stakes are high on both sides of the law enforcement equation. Violence is common — three men were killed in a shootout on the night we were there.

We found a similarly heavy atmosphere prevailing in the regions of Mexico adjacent to the border. President Vincente Fox has been under a good deal of pressure from the Bush administration to deal with the movements of illegal migrants and narcotics, and his policemen — packing major heat in the form of side-arms and automatic assault rifles — are out to scare the pants off anyone who thinks he has a reason to approach the Rio Grande from the Mexican side.

Along the border there were hundreds of wooden crosses hanging in the hurricane wire, a poignant reminder to would-be wetbacks of the fate of their *compañeros* who didn't quite make it, drowning in the river or baking to death in shipping containers in which they were abandoned by the driver hired to smuggle them when the authorities came sniffing around.

We could see at a glance why there's such pressure on the border from the Mexican side — as soon as you're across, standards of living drop as dramatically as the body mass index of the people you pass. The landscape south of the border is arid and poor, and so are the people who work it. The buildings are shanties at best, the farmers as scrawny and weathered as their livestock. The majority of Mexicans live subsistence lifestyles; there's real, grinding poverty everywhere you look. Little wonder your average Mexican will jump at any faint chance to make it across the border to the Land of Opportunity, where they can lead a better life and improve the lives of family back home.

The United States has suffered a series of marked mood swings on the question of Mexican immigration over the years. The first great wave of migration wasn't strictly migration at all. Instead, the border was shifted south. After the United States defeated Mexico in their little contretemps in the 1840s, a vast amount of Mexican territory — the entire states of California and Texas and good proportions of Colorado, Arizona, New Mexico, Utah and Nevada — was ceded to the victor for a paltry $15 million under the terms of the 1848 Treaty of Guadalupe Hidalgo. Another vast tract was added in 1864, when the southern portions of Arizona and New Mexico were bought by the United States from the Mexican government in what is known as the Gadsden Purchase. These two measures increased the territory of the United States by one third.

The citizens of these formerly Mexican territories, needless to say, suddenly became United States citizens. Over the years many thousands of their compadres south of the new border sought to join them. After the Mexican revolution in 1900, which encouraged many more Mexicans to slip north of the border permanently, and before the United States government embarked on a campaign to repatriate Americans of Mexican origin during the Depression of the 1930s, the population of Mexican-born Americans tripled.

For a time during the early 1940s, as American involvement in World War II created a labour shortage, Mexican labour was encouraged to step into the gap. No sooner had the war ended, however, than the welcome mat was rolled up and another round of expulsions began, lasting well into the 1950s when the notorious Operation Wetback got underway, the equivalent of Piggy Muldoon's dawn raids on Polynesian overstayers in New Zealand.

The latest drift to *el norte* from Mexico began in the 1970s. There were 800,000 Mexican Americans in the United States in 1970. Though no one is sure exactly how many there are today, it's thought there are about 20 million. Mexico is by far the highest contributor to United States immigration, both legal and illegal. The official estimates are that 60 per cent of illegal immigrants on United States soil, some seven million souls, are Mexican, although most commentators reckon that figure is deeply conservative. Such is the predominance of Mexicans in the statistics that illegal immigrants are reported in two categories: Mexican and Other Than Mexican. And the problem continues to grow, with half a million Mexicans trying their luck at getting across every year.

Until 2006 the last glimmer of official compassion for illegal immigration by Mexicans came in 1986 when an amnesty was declared, allowing those present in the United States illegally to remain stateside so long as they came forward and made themselves known to the census people and, of course, to the Inland Revenue Service. Around a third of them did. Since then popular opinion and public policy has hardened against the rising Hispanic tide. In the 1990s a crackdown on the most popular crossing points slashed the numbers of intending illegal immigrants arrested at the border — and sent soaring the numbers attempting to cross at wilder points of the long border, along with the death toll. It's thought that 300 to 400 lose their lives each year in their bid to answer the Statue of Liberty's call.

Meanwhile, there's plenty of work for those who do get through. Without the Hispanic labour force, Californian agriculture would collapse and fat, lazy Americans everywhere would have to do the dirty, menial jobs they consider beneath themselves.

That's given rise to the curious, contradictory rhetoric you'll hear in official circles about the Mexican wave of immigration. On one hand you've got the Washington wing of the Republican Party promising to crack down on the 'problem'. On the other you've got the Gubernator, Californian state governor Arnold Schwarzenegger, himself hopeful for a future Republican presidential nomination, coughing uncomfortably and proposing to allow illegal Mexican immigrants to obtain driver's licences in his state. (Without them, half the well-off white children of California are being driven to school by unlicensed drivers.)

Schwarzenegger was an immigrant himself. He played the melting-pot card for all it was worth in his electoral campaign, reminding everyone that he had arrived in the United States from his native Austria with his pockets empty and his head full of dreams. Once he was elected, however, he was at pains to ensure no one imagined that he meant that Mexicans were worth chucking in the melting pot — heads full of dreams or not. Pull up the ladder, Jack.

The current thrust of United States policy toward illegal Mexican immigrants can be summed up thus: stay out, but if you make it in, come do my dishes, look after my babies and spray my crops. As recently as 2006, this schizophrenia was underlined when Mr Bush ordered 6000 state troopers to the border to help stem the flow of illegals, yet announced at the same time what amounted to an amnesty for the twelve million illegals already living and working stateside. He also spoke of a 'guest worker' programme that would allow people to enter the United States and work temporarily, freeing up a flow of cheap labour for American manufacturing.

The spectre of thousands of state troopers manning the border with Mexico didn't quite match the impression we had once we crossed back to the United States from Mexico and were riding along the northern banks of the Rio Grande. Indeed, we were struck by just how empty the landscape was, and couldn't quite reconcile this reality with the television images of armed patrols racing up and down along the border line. All we could see was a piddly stream separating the First and the Third worlds. Seized by a sudden nostalgia for Mexico we parked the bikes, took a good look around for Barney Fife, Andy Griffith and the rest of the National Guard who we had chewed the fat with at the official checkpoint, then stripped off and dived into the warm, easily flowing water. We struck out for the far bank and within ten strokes touched the sand of Mexico. So easy.

From what we've learnt about immigration in our travels, it's hard enough to get by in a foreign country with money and documents, let alone buck naked and with nothing to your name. So there were clearly limited prospects for us in Mexico.

Reluctantly, we turned and stroked back to the United States, planting our footprints on American soil as wetbacks. We dried off quickly in the desert heat, got dressed and resumed our journey.

Later, when we mentioned this stunt to Texas locals, they were quite incredulous. They couldn't believe we hadn't been shot at or thrown into the back of a paddywagon and trundled off to the clink. We told them they shouldn't believe everything they see on television and they told us to keep our little escapade quiet. Americans, it seems, or at least Americans in the border regions, come without a sense of humour on this particular subject.

TEX MEX

Just south of the Mexican border it was as though the lights had come on again. There's something about biking in the Third World — crappy roads, awful driving, life-threatening encounters with huge, speeding trucks on blind corners, dismal landscapes, language difficulties, dubious food hygiene standards . . . ah, that's where it's at.

First thing we noticed was the heat. It was searing and, while you might think the last thing you'd want is your head enclosed in a full-face motorcycle helmet in 46 degrees Celsius, it's much preferred to having your skin flayed by the hot breeze. We wore our BMW rally jackets with the thermal linings stripped out and Icebreaker merino vests soaked in water underneath. This was a trick we'd learned on the Silk Road. Dave, who had been sceptical, had tried it on a subsequent trip to Australia and was now a convert.

The countryside was spectacular and strangely familiar. It

could have been a movie set for a Western, with tall cacti dotting the dry sands just as they do in every John Wayne movie you've ever watched. The land was marginal at best for farming but farm it they did. The leathery, deeply tanned locals leaned wearily on their hand tools to watch as we rode by. Donkeys, the universal mode of transport in the developing world, were everywhere, just as they had been throughout Central Asia. We found it hard to reconcile this with where we'd just come from — the land of John Deere combine harvesters creeping side-by-side across vast tracts of cropland.

The next thing we noticed was the food. After the crap we'd been eating on commercial premises in El Norte, the simple Mexican fare was nectar of the gods. American food is disgusting. We quickly learned that when we ordered practically any dish at a restaurant we had to instruct them to 'hold the cheese'. We learned this the hard way by suffering through dishes that were smothered in it. We like cheese but not American cheese, nasty processed stuff that it is, flexible, slightly glossy and incredibly tenacious. Dave and Gareth amused themselves while trying to eat a plate of nachos by picking the cheese off and rolling it into balls. Jo had to intervene to stop them stoning the chef with cheeseballs.

Everything in the United States — probably including the cheese — has sugar in it, even the white bread. And the tragic consequences of it are all too plain to see. It's not uncommon to see a big clutch of mobility scooters parked up outside the donut shop. Their owners' affliction? Too many bloody donuts. You hear talk of the looming obesity problem New Zealand is facing; America has got it, full-blown.

Our second day in the desert took us to the remarkable springs at Cuatro Ciénegas, something like Takaka's Pupu Springs right in the middle of the arid waste of the desert. We had a heavenly swim there, skylarking about in the warm, clear, blue water while the land around us shimmered with mirages.

The third day was one of the most gruelling to date — 440 km in extreme heat as we hauled up the Sierra Madre Occidentale, the great mountain range between the Mexican desert and the Pacific coast. Half of it was on a pretty fair road surface that we had practically to ourselves. Of course, we'd paid $20 in tolls for the privilege, way too steep for most of the locals. By late afternoon, however, the character of the road changed. We began the 63 km descent to Batopilas, a small town at the bottom of one of the Copper Canyons, great chasms in the Sierra Madre strongly reminiscent of the Grand Canyon. As we negotiated the narrow, bumpy road around dozens of sharp hairpins that formed the switchbacks on the canyon walls, it felt as though that yawning drop was just one ill-judged cornering manoeuvre away. It was a pretty good test of our upright skills. It reminded us of a road at La Paz, reputed to be the world's most dangerous, that we once tackled in a fit of madness on bicycles. No disrespect to the Copper Canyon, the La Paz descent was more than 3500 metres — close to the height of Mount Cook!

We took the Copper Canyon road quietly, stopping every so often for the photo opportunities afforded by the breath-taking vistas. We all made it down safely although Roger managed a contretemps with a culvert and a canyon wall, leaving him with a graze to the hand which he tried to hide from Dave, who had earlier wagged his head when he saw Roger removing his gloves in the heat and strongly advised him to wear them. After that we moved to a state of heightened alert over the tendency of the loose metal to coax you into the ditches and over the edges. No harm done though, apart from Roger's hand, and we finished off the day drinking beer with the Stetson-wearing locals at a Batopilas inn. Man, had we earned our Coronas!

Batopilas is something of a burnt-out boomtown, very pretty, with the Spanish architecture of its glory days quite well preserved. At its peak, when the nearby silver mine was one of the richest in the world, there were 7000 inhabitants. These days, there are only about 800. Nestled as it is at the bottom of the canyon, it has a distinct microclimate — tropical fruit such as banana, avocado, mango and papaya flourish here, even though you're likely to see snow capping the canyon rim in winter. It's pretty cool, complete with a 17th century triple-domed Jesuit mission church.

This is Tarahumara Indian country and we enjoyed learning about these extraordinary people. Among the young spivs with their arms dangling from the windows of their Chevy pickup trucks and the cowboys riding down the main street of the town on prancing horses with beautifully tooled Spanish saddles, we spotted a Tarahumara bloke just as proudly strolling along in his loincloth.

As on the Silk Road, interest in us, our bikes and our proposed route mapped out on our panniers was intense. Every time we stopped we'd soon acquire a crowd of people of all ages who we'd experiment upon with our atrocious Spanish. Jo did somewhat better than the rest of us, and

Dave was a hit with the kids — just like on the Silk Road.

The ride up and out of the great canyon was no less hairy than the descent — a little worse if anything, because we knew what to expect. We tackled it early and were rewarded with a beautiful sunrise.

The following day we made a round trip from our digs in Creel, high in the Sierra, to Divisadero, which gives fantastic views of the canyon of Urique. At 1860 m deep, this is the deepest of the Copper Canyons, deeper in fact than the Grand Canyon. The scale of it is almost too much to appreciate, with the town of Urique way below us at the end of another of those demanding roads.

The pair of us and Dave stopped at a suitable vantage point to await the return of Roger, who'd got ahead of us. While we were waiting, we reasoned, we may as well make ourselves comfortable. Gareth set up his iPod to play through his portable speakers and soon we had an Indian war dance blaring out over the dusty landscape. Jo had a billy on the Primus and before she really knew what was going on she found Dave and Gareth stripped to their underpants prancing in a circle around her, whooping and clapping their hands over their mouths, redskin-style. She just shook her head and went on sprinkling tea leaves into the billy.

The temperature climbed appreciably as we dropped on the way down from the Sierra to Cuauhtémoc, on the fringes of the Chihuahua Desert. Here our Spanish was of limited use as the town was a Mennonite colony and its inhabitants spoke Old German. We had reason to stop at a family-run machine shop where we procured a bolt for a loose pannier and, despite the language difference, the transaction was conducted effortlessly — especially since they gave it to us gratis. While we were there Jo noticed the curtains of the house twitching as whoever was inside worked out what the moral hazards of the space aliens that had just landed outside her house might be. It reminded her of moments on our Silk Road tour where the women in strict Islamic societies would hesitate to make contact with us.

Sure enough, just as it often happened in Muslim countries, the door eventually opened and a portly woman in a long purple dress and with immaculately parted hair restrained by a black bonnet emerged with her similarly clad daughter. The language was a barrier but we managed to persuade them to sit on the motorbikes. They made for quite a sight, astride the latest technology yet dressed in their 1940s 'sensible' ankle-length and neck-to-wrist, country dancing, good-girl dresses.

Like the Amish, the Mennonites are floundering at the shallow end of their gene pool because of the lack of recruits. We saw the Amish had adopted Korean children in an effort to reduce the risk of congenital diseases; in Cuanhtémoc we spoke to a young Mennonite lady who had been shipped down here from Canada to freshen the bloodlines a little.

We spent our last day in Mexico with our tongues hanging out in the intense heat of the Chihuahua Desert, where the blinding white gypsum sands reflect the sun mercilessly. The only shelter available was in the odd roadside shrine, doubtless erected to protect pilgrims from the heat. We parked up in the shade of one of these while Gareth did one of his radio interviews with Paul Holmes.

It didn't help that we'd all by now reverted to that other

normal condition of travellers in the Third World — the squirts. Somehow, despite all precautions, Montezuma's Revenge always finds you out. It's all part of the experience and a small price to pay. We wouldn't swap it for anything.

AMERICAN BY NATURE

Our first meaningful interaction with the wildlife of America was in the Bahamas. Jo had been warned by the locals and wore insect repellent but the boys were dismissive when she tried to pass the warnings on. Consequently, they spent the first couple of weeks of the trip scratching at itches from the bites of a bug the Bahamans call 'no see-ums'. For obvious reasons we can't tell you what they look like.

One thing none of us was prepared for was the profusion and diversity of the wildlife we got to see in America, which most people — us included, before we went — tend to regard as an urban jungle interspersed with cattle ranches and wheat fields. And it wasn't just in the parks, wilderness areas and wildlife preserves — it seems you can build over their habitat all you like but the tenacious critters of America will find a way of coexisting with you. In practically any green area in the towns or cities you'd catch a flicker of movement out of the corner of your eye and, if you were quick enough, spot a squirrel darting up a tree. Signs at most of the motels where we stopped insisted that we were not to feed the raccoons. These little varmints bear a passing resemblance to our own pesky possums except they have a black stripe like a Beagle Boys burglar mask across their eyes. They're cute but they make a hell of a mess of unsecured rubbish sacks and trash cans — or the backpacks and panniers of unwary travellers.

We weren't long on the road in Florida before we began to see armadillos, which we christened possums-in-a-half-shell, mostly splattered on the carriageway. In fact much of our early appreciation of the profusion and diversity of American wildlife was gained through observation of what was pancaked on the blacktops: everything from tiddlers such as squirrels, armadillos, raccoons, snakes and small alligators to medium-sized critters such as foxes, pigs, coyotes and larger alligators to big critters such as deer and full-size alligators.

When we rode the Shenandoah Parkway in the Appalachians we were warned by locals to keep a weather eye out for white-tailed deer, which have a habit of leaping from the undergrowth at the roadside with no warning or standing frozen like possums in your headlight when you round a corner at night. There's an important difference between possums and deer though — body mass. The rider's not going to come out of it too well when you go bike versus deer. We saw few deer but several groundhogs — a kind of big, fat, outsized ginger guinea pig — and lots of squirrels, possums and armadillos, alive and dead, as well as eagles riding the air currents above on their tassel-tipped wings.

One day we were nearing the end of another parkway, the Natchez Trace — the old Choctaw Indian and then European traders' route down the Mississippi River from Nashville to Baton Rouge. We were being guided by one of the locals on an old Honda when we saw a turtle toddling along in the middle of the carriageway between fields of sugarcane, alongside one of the levees that keep the Mississippi (mostly) in its place. We pulled over and went to examine it a bit more closely and get it over to the side of the road and out of harm's way. Closer examination showed it to have a mean-looking mouth and a whole lot of attitude shining out of its lidless, reptilian eyes, like some ill-tempered nonagenarian. It didn't pull in its head the way you expect of turtles and tortoises; instead it took a great big air-shot at us with its jaws.

We were manhandling it to the verge — it was pretty heavy, though not as big as they get (these suckers can grow to 180 kg and a metre across) — when a ute hove into view and pulled calmly over to where the bikes were parked.

It takes American policemen a time to get themselves out of their vehicles, doubtless because they have to unsnag all the pistols, batons, pepper sprays and cuffs that dangle from their utility belts and hook up on things in the vehicle's interior. And somehow it always seems to take longer in the South. As this portly lawman — the deputy sheriff of the district, as it turned out — performed the manoeuvre, we were wondering what wildlife protection ordinance we were infringing by bothering the turtle.

'That there's an alligator snapping turtle,' the man drawled. 'What y'all fixin' to do with it?'

'We were just moving it to the side of the road,' replied Jo.

'So it didn't get hurt.'

'Y' expect me to believe y'all had no intention of removin' it from the area?'

We shook our heads.

'Well, then,' he said. 'Y'all won't mind handin' it over.'

We cooperated and put the turtle into the back of his pickup.

'They go awful nice with sauce,' he explained.

Having saved the old girl from the marauding wheels of semi-trailer trucks, we wondered whether we should intervene here too. But there was a pistol in that holster.

The turtle safely stowed in the tray, the lawman came over and studied the maps on our panniers and interrogated us — in the nicest possible way — about our trip, where we'd been, where we were going. He offered us maps, told us he had a key to the historic church in a nearby town and offered to take us on a guided tour. But we were behind schedule so we had to thank him and let him keep his date with turtle soup without us.

Much of the wildlife is a menace. When we visited Cape Canaveral, we learned that alligators were pretty common in the area but that attacks were rare. Who knows what it is about us but we seem to have a knack on these trips of ours of arriving on the scene immediately before disaster; very shortly after our visit, a trainee astronaut was bitten by a gator while jogging around the compound.

We kept a lookout for them. We stayed one night in a trapper's hut just outside Gibson, Louisiana, built on stilts over the water of the bayou. It was great, set among dank, drooping, dripping foliage, with mist drifting through the canopy. We didn't need the locals to assure us that this was gator country. But where were they? The largest living creature that made itself immediately obvious was a pretty albino peacock.

Jo liberally ladled fish guts she had brought specially from the coast into the brooding brown waters, which certainly brought the turtles from miles around. No gators at first but soon enough a swirl in the water and the flick of a knobbly, muscular tail indicated they were on the job. They were tiddlers at first but before long all those snapping jaws and stumpy, flailing limbs became slightly unsettling. Each one that happened along was bigger than the last. Alligators are a slightly sleepier, less aggressive proposition than the saltwater crocs they have in Australia but make no mistake, alligators are dangerous. One look at their crooked, toothy grin and we had no doubt they could be very bad for our health.

We slept that night plagued by squadrons of twin-engined mosquitoes, hearing the occasional swish, slap and scrape of gators threading through the piles beneath the hut. Needless to say, no one was game for a dip in the morning.

The following day we got closer to one than was prudent and Jo took the whole Steve Irwin gator-baiting thing a bit far. With terrifying speed the critter locked its jaws on her hand — lucky it was only 30 cm long. A mild infection set in but soon cleared up, so there was no need to leave the rest of her for the bigger gators. Still, it made for a good posting on the blog. No sooner had we announced that Jo had been bitten by an alligator than we were inundated with frantic messages of concern from family, friends and devoted followers of the *Backblocks* enterprise.

Probably the closest we came to having a genuinely nasty brush with the wildlife came when we went to check into a seedy motel in Batopilas, at the bottom of one of the Copper Canyons in Mexico's Sierra Madre. A young Mexican man preceded Dave and Roger into their room. There was a scream and he suddenly exited in a state of high agitation, speaking rapid Spanish and gesturing back through the doorway.

"Ees snake, señors," the proprietor explained. "He see snake. Ees no problem."

He fetched a blunt instrument of some sort and went into the room. After a few muffled thuds and curses, he emerged sweeping the offending reptile out with a broom. It was small — about 60 cm — and black with bright red and yellow rings. This, we later learned, was a coral snake, one with a neurotoxic venom that paralyses your central nervous system as it holds on with its fangs long after sinking them in — just the tonic for tired bikers lying back on their beds to relax after a hard day's ride.

'Ees fixed,' he beamed, but by now our enthusiasm for his establishment had cooled. We found Juanita's Hotel just down the road and, while it seemed a cut above the first joint, we all checked under our beds and in the dark corners of the wardrobes pretty thoroughly before turning in for the night. Apart from the pigs scoffing any detritus emerging from the hotel's waste pipes, it was positively civilised.

Bears gave us pause for thought too. It took a while before we got to see one. It was Gareth who first saw a black bear, a long way off in the distance across a grasslands plain in Yellowstone National Park. He maxed the zoom on his camera to 12x and then digitally zoomed on top of that to get his 'close-up' — a rather blurry furry. But within five minutes of performing this feat of technological exaggeration, he was face to face with another bear that was ripping the innards from a fallen log in search of morsels. A park ranger wasn't far behind to shoo Gareth on his way, leaving the bear to his solitude. Soon everyone had seen a bear, except Dave. Everyone told their exciting bear stories, swapping notes on the paradox of these creatures, which for all their cuddly appearance had such a fearsome reputation — except Dave. The miles rolled by, with the bear-infested wilderness passing on either side. We saw more bears, padding along in the distance or peering shyly from the woods at the roadside. The rest of us were getting pretty much bored with bears but Dave still hadn't even spotted his first. It was starting to get to him.

Finally he came across one out on the verge. It scrutinised us for a long moment then ducked down out of sight. We didn't think much more of it but then movement nearby caught our eye. There, silently and as if from nowhere, the bear had reappeared, only a few dozen metres away. Talking to locals later, we learned that this is typical bear behaviour. They're unpredictable and, for all their bulk, capable of amazing stealth. Undaunted, Dave started following it down the road, click, click, clicking away to make up for his paucity of bear shots. Indeed, he got closer to it than any of the rest of us would have cared to, such was his exhilaration.

At a place in British Columbia called Bell 2 — so-named, we were told, because something catastrophic had happened to the original Bell — a truckload of rifle-toting men in baseball caps and checked shirts hauled in. They were off into the mountains to look for their buddy, they told us, who had disappeared the previous year. Their suspicion was that he'd fallen foul of a bear somewhere.

One of the highlights of our bear-watching came one day in the Canadian Rockies when Gareth stopped to take a photo of a Wakatipu-type lake scene. Turning around to return to his bike parked on the other side of the road, he looked up to see a mother grizzly right there in the meadow by the bike with her two young 'uns. Now this was a big bear, and the grizzly is the hardest species to get near. This one was close — strictly speaking, a little too close for comfort. Thankfully, he'd left his bike going so even as he busily click, click, clicked and mama bear got down on all fours, and then each of the babies did the same, he was swiftly calculating whether he'd beat her in a flat sprint to the bike, which was on its stand about halfway between them. Eventually the three bears ambled into the undergrowth and Gareth roared off happily, confident he'd scored the best bear shots of the trip to date.

We were warned not to camp any further north than Fairbanks, Alaska, on our way to Deadhorse, the North Pole of our expedition, because the bears wouldn't be able to resist the temptation of tents that were so well-stocked with bear food — both our supplies and ourselves (we were assured Big Ted wouldn't discriminate).

In late July we camped out in Yosemite National Park and woke to find that a Mustang convertible parked no more than 100 m from our tents had been broken into, the rear window ripped out of the soft-top. Honestly, some people have no respect for other people's property — and nor do bears, when they spy an unattended sandwich on your back seat. The paw prints on the paintwork of the fenders gave the culprit away: a bear, probably a black or a brown, had torn its way in to get at a burger left in all its olfactory glory by the unwary driver. The park staff left a notice on the car telling them what went down and inviting them to write for an official incident report for insurance purposes. They dish out hundreds of these notices every year, as the bears in the park have learned what a treasure trove cars can be and have quite a sophisticated theft-ex-auto racket running.

As you'd expect, the wildlife preserves and the national parks boasted the most prolific fauna. As we followed the Rocky Mountains northward from the Four Corners and the temperature fell, the scenic quotient went right up. (The Four Corners is a point where the borders of four states — Arizona, Utah, Colorado and New Mexico — form a cross, and where we played a game resembling Twister to touch the ground of all four states at once.)

We had a beautiful night's camping at nearly 3000 m at the Cedar Breaks National Monument. There were deer and marmot everywhere and although there were rumours of a resident bear we never saw it. The ranger who warned us about it showed great interest in our bikes and our trip and vowed to treat us to trout for dinner. Off he went with a rod, boasting of the park's angling bounty and his own prowess with a fly. We had noodles and beer for tea.

Wyoming's Yellowstone, probably the best-known of America's national parks, was lovely, even if the wonders that wow Americans — the geysers and mud pools — are a little passé for travellers from a land that boasts Whakarewarewa. We saw deer and bears galore, and bison. Nothing you see on a beef or dairy unit in New Zealand quite prepares you for these ancient-looking, great-headed, shaggy-bearded monsters. We'd seen bigger beasts — water buffalo — on the subcontinent but they're pretty placid compared with bison, which kill more people each year in Yellowstone than bears do. Despite their clumsy appearance and large size, at a gallop they can exceed the New Zealand speed limit for a built-up area. No one could really tell us how they felt about motorbikes. For these reasons, when we saw them grazing by the side of the road, we proceeded with a fair measure of caution.

Strangely, though, the greatest danger in Yellowstone wasn't the wildlife: it was the people gawking at the wildlife. You'd come around a corner to find yourself confronted with the tailgate of the last SUV in a line of SUVs parked at crazy angles all over the carriageway, while their owners snapped away at bison or whatever other critters had poked their heads from the shrubbery.

Bison have come back from the brink. By the beginning of the 20th century they were all but gone, with only a few hundred head left. The Indians had hunted them but never really possessed the technology to threaten their survival. Their most destructive technique was for braves

— and we use the term advisedly — to drive them along races constructed of willows and grass to cliff edges and then select the choice cuts from the slab at the bottom, but even this hardly dented their numbers. Nevertheless, it's been suggested that the introduction of the horse actually boosted the numbers of bison, as greater mobility meant the hunter of the family could keep up with them and shoot and take only what he needed.

Europeans were less discriminating. When they twigged to the fact that the Plains Indian tribes were dependent on the bison for their subsistence, the railroad companies wasted no time in engaging professional hunters to exterminate them, confident that this would encourage those pesky Injuns to move along. It did. Even when the professional hunters, such as William 'Buffalo Bill' Cody, started asking for protection for the pitiful remnants of the bison herds, the anti-Indian interests in Washington overruled them. By the time the hunting had finished, numbers of the American bison were down to a few hundred nationwide.

Yellowstone boasts the only continuously wild herd of bison in the United States (the only other such herd is in Canada). The current herd has recovered from its all-time low of 23 to now number about 3500, enough to begin to spill out of the park boundary and bother ranchers, who insist they carry cattle diseases. Elsewhere, their numbers have also rebounded, largely thanks to concerted conservation efforts. But few bison today are the pure-bred descendants of the great herds that roamed the prairie; most have been admixed with introduced domestic cattle somewhere along the line.

With all this prey around, it was inevitable we'd see more sign of predators as well. We saw coyote roadkill one day, a beige dog about the size of a small Alsatian with a set of wicked-looking teeth on display in its death grimace. It wasn't until 50 km down the road that it occurred to Jo that those fangs would make a handsome necklace. It was far too late to go back but she began to take a much more predatory interest in roadkill.

A couple of days later Gareth came upon Jo and Dave crouching by the roadside, intent on something. Worried that someone might be hurt or that there was some mechanical reason for their attentions, he stopped, only to find they were using a Leatherman multi-tool to perform dental extractions on a mostly two-dimensional porcupine. The hollow spines of this very dead piece of roadkill managed to penetrate Dave's heavy biker's boots and were still there a couple of days later and had to be extracted with pliers. Apparently they are a collector's piece, used in the manufacture of native American jewellery. As our trip proceeded we learned more and more of the treasure trove that is roadkill.

Coyotes used to be more or less confined to the Pacific Northwest of America but human habitation has helped them spread right across North America. They're cunning, resourceful and adapt easily to the streetwise urban lifestyle of the stray dog. We heard coyotes quite frequently when camping out at night: a high, mournful howl or a series of yips. Both calls send a bit of a shiver down your spine but they're not much to be afraid of. Funnily enough, they're more of a threat in towns and cities where they can get aggro if the supply of rubbish, cats and lapdogs dries up. They're not exactly flavour of the month with American farmers, who are obliged to factor losses to coyotes into their stock management. In the Carolinas we saw a cow of some sort — even Dave couldn't help us with the breed — with a great, spreading set of evil-looking horns. She was well capable, you might think, of looking after herself and hers yet she was mourning the loss of her calf to a coyote.

Gareth finally saw one, fleetingly, soon afterwards in the Canadian Rockies. The coyote was there at the roadside for a moment and then it was gone, like a grey ghost.

While he may have been the unluckiest bear hunter among us, Dave was the only one to be favoured with a glimpse of a lynx. He had seen what he thought was a deer crossing the road ahead and had slowed down to see where it had disappeared to in the woods. There it was, a big, mean pussycat with tufted ears and no tail, sat atop a rock just staring at him. With camera already out, he got away only one good shot before the cat retreated into the undergrowth. But he had his proof and we were all mightily impressed.

A s the human population thinned from the Canadian Rockies and north into British Columbia, the Yukon and Alaska, the wildlife was fantastic. If the east of America, with forest lining the beautiful parkways, was heavily wooded then this territory was something else again. We spent days and days riding through woodlands, towered over by immense pine, spruce and fir trees. Even Dave was bored with bear sightings by now. There were deer everywhere too and we saw elk, which Kiwis know as wapiti and which are not to be confused with European elk, actually the same as North American moose. Confusing? You bet.

The moose remained elusive all the way up the Rocky Mountains until the second to last day of our traverse of Canadian territory. We were riding in the rain up the Stewart-Cassiar 'Highway', a decidedly second-tier road that traverses the coastal mountain range of British Columbia before crossing into the Yukon. MoD spotted one, with its blunt nose and hunched shoulders, on the other side of a lagoon. A little further on, at the aptly named Moose Meadow, we spotted several moose with calves wading across a lake and feeding on the waterlilies. The calves were certainly getting an early swimming lesson. That same lake showed us a busy beaver tending its dam and the first of many bald eagles, the symbol of America, perched atop a conifer nearby.

Once distributed right across North America, the bald eagle was on the endangered list in the United States for most of the 20th century. Intensive conservation efforts have brought it back to the point where removing it from the list is a real possibility. It was always more plentiful in Canada. Of the 70,000 American birds, about half live in Alaska, most around Haines, as we were to find out. Little wonder then that the sight of these magnificent birds had all but lost its novelty by the time we returned from Alaska and were well down the Pacific coast.

The best moose encounter we had was when Gareth surprised a big bull with its head underwater munching on plants in a shallow creek just north of Haines. It raised its dripping head, shot him a startled look over its shoulder as he levelled his camera, then plunged its head back underwater and went right on eating.

It wasn't just in the national parks and the woodlands that we encountered American wildlife. Even in the deserts and the frozen wastes of Alaska there was plenty to see. The spring melt in Alaska turns the entire state into a wetland for the summer, with the underground permafrost forming an impenetrable basin. Caribou were everywhere, along with wading and waddling birds of all description. A fox came poking around our morning-tea stop on the way up the Prudhoe Bay road to the Arctic Ocean. Jo got the fright of her life the night we spent at Deadhorse, Prudhoe Bay. She was stalking a caribou by the light of the midnight sun, keeping down low, camera in hand, moving cautiously along the side of a huge tracked vehicle parked near the outskirts of the settlement, where it fades into the tundra. She was intent on her prey but at the back of her mind were the stories of the rogue polar bear said by locals to haunt the location. As she reached the end of the vehicle she noticed movement from the corner of her eye. She whirled to face the danger and found herself confronted by an equally startled camera-toting Dave Wallace, who'd been sneaking up the other side of the same vehicle.

'What are you doing out here?' he gasped. 'It's the middle of the night! It's not safe!'

Nor was the tundra quite the dull grassland you might expect. Summer brings it alive with flowers of an amazing range of colours, especially a vivid pink bloom named fireweed.

Then there were the 3500-year-old bristlecone pine trees up in Kootenay National Park, British Columbia, still thriving at an altitude of 3000 m. Here Roger and Gareth were startled by two elk the size of houses bounding across in front of their bikes and effortlessly hurdling the 'deer-proof' fence that lined the road.

The desert regions lower down were fertile in their own way, with the various succulent and spiky plants that have adapted to the waterless regions putting on a show. Similarly in Death Valley, Arizona, where you'd expect there to be no life whatsoever, we found a particularly fetching plant, a low shrub with spiky white leaves like holly carved from ice. The pale foliage, you'd suppose, reflects the bulk of the sunlight and protects it from excessive evaporation. The desert will also throw up the occasional coyote yip and is host to gopher, rabbit, hare, and roadrunner.

I n the main the wildlife was under threat from only our cameras, although, as noted previously, Dave proved himself to be the scourge of the Alaskan salmon fishery. We spent three days watching wildlife and trying to drink the bar dry on a ferry on the Inner Passage, one of the routes of the Alaska Marine Highway System. These are passenger and vehicular ferries that integrate with the roading system in such a way as to make travel possible even when the parts of Alaska you want to reach are frozen solid. The three-day trip from Haines in Alaska to Port Hardy on Vancouver Island passed through some of the world's prettiest scenery, not unlike coastal Fiordland. There was also a huge variety of marine life, including seals and humpback whales. The sight of these immense creatures breaching or waving their tail flukes in the air is breathtaking.

Still, three days is a long time to do nothing but sit on a boat, stare at the scenery and get drunk. By the time we reached Port Hardy we were more than ready to get back in the saddle.

THE ROAD
LEADS BACK TO YOU

One of the drawcards of the southern states was its rich musical heritage. Few music-loving New Zealanders would have escaped falling under the spell of at least one of the genres of music this region has produced, including jazz, the blues, bluegrass and rock'n'roll. It's some kind of phenomenon that all were born or shaped within spitting distance of the Mississippi Delta. Our own exploration of this aspect of American culture was a must.

What's more, music is an integral part of motorcycle touring. We both have iPods and at times we squeeze the little button earpieces under our helmets — we call singing along in the privacy of your own protective headgear 'helmet karaoke'. Plenty of this went down on our tour of the United States, courtesy of a playlist Gareth set up before we left.

As we rode north from Florida we were humming along to *Carolina in My Mind*. Pennsylvania and the Flight 93 memorial saw us in Boss country so we were belting out

Springsteen's *Born in the USA* as the sun gradually warmed our numb fingers. And while we were all probably thinking *Duelling Banjos* as we rode the Shenandoah Parkway in the Appalachians, it was *Take Me Home, Country Roads* we were listening to. Georgia is rich pickings for those trying to score a road trip soundtrack. Naturally we had *Georgia On My Mind* on our minds.

We all knew the words to *The Ballad of Davy Crockett* for our visit to the great man's birthplace but we came away unable, try as we might, to shake the Woody Woodpecker ditty from our heads. Thanks a bunch, Dave.

But the core genre of United States music is country and we were drowned in it in Tennessee. First it was Nashville's Country Music Hall of Fame, which these days is a broad church, laying claim to a wide range of musicians from Elvis to Ray Charles and all the country singers in between. Johnny Cash and Willie Nelson, both of whom collaborated with Charles to fuse his Chicago blues with the hillbilly gospel roots of Elvis and produce populist pap, were of course included too.

We got a raw experience of the all-American phenomenon that is country music when we attended a gig at the Grand Ole Opry in Nashville. This started out as the WSM Barn Dance, a live music broadcast from the premises of an insurance company in 1925, but somewhere along the way it acquired its current name (from 'Grand Opera') and an immense following. Many fans came to Nashville and demanded to see the acts live.

The Grand Ole Opry outgrew the insurance company in 1943 and 30 years later moved to its present premises, an auditorium not unlike a tennis stadium. It draws huge, adoring crowds, as it did on the night we visited, and it still goes out live on television and radio right across America.

We sat through a number of songs in the Hank Williams tradition with a bit of the Carter family thrown in but were most entertained by the 'Cracker Barrel' family restaurant ads that the compere would regularly break into between acts. These had us in fits even though we knew it was still a live radio show.

Then suddenly the night was transformed. No sooner had six-foot-six Trace Adkins taken the stage than it was obvious that this was who the crowd had come to see. Dozens of females in the crowd rushed the stage while others just went wild. Everything from flowers to scraps of lingerie began descending on the stage from the bleachers. It was like a Beatles concert in 1963. Adkins is a broad bloke with long hair swept back in a ponytail and a deep, deep gravelly voice. As he pulsated through his cameo, *Ladies Love Country Boys*, the audience was transformed from one of polite, respectful rednecks to a raging torrent of hysterical adoration. Trace certainly knew how to flick their switches.

Ever heard of Trace? Well, Trace symbolises what the South stands for — big as a Chevy pickup, been arrested for drink-driving, lost a finger on an industrial site, sang at the Republican Party's national convention and belted out the national anthem at the 2006 World Series final. He's a staunch George W Bush supporter and drinks only beer. Trace makes Bruce Springsteen look like Boy George and the Ayatollah Khomeini like Mr Bean.

***

Surrounded by the mass hysteria of the Nashville womenfolk, Gareth looked at Roger and raised his eyebrows. Roger spread his hands and shrugged. Jo stayed tightly focused on the pelvic action going down (and up) on stage. The bloke's set — musical set, that is — was impressive. Even the boys had a tear in their eye during some of his numbers — laughter can do that. For us, the Beatlemania seemed a little out of proportion. But that's because we don't know country. Sixty per cent of music sales in the United States are of country music.

It's been said that country music is 'three chords and the truth', 'music to beat your wife by' and 'tales of divorce, dogs and dying'. It's also been said that if you play a country record backwards, the singer gets a job, his wife comes back and his dog comes back to life. But when Trace broke out his *I Like My Women a Little on the Trashy Side* we thought the crowd was going to trash the auditorium upholstery.

You can think or say what you like about it but country music is the soundtrack of middle America. Never heard of Garth Brooks either? That's hardly likely to bother Garth. The country icon has sold 115 million albums to the faithful in the United States. And Texas country act the Dixie Chicks sold $49 million worth of concert tickets in a single day in those happier times before they stuck their necks out to criticise the war in Iraq.

Alcohol abuse might be tolerated by the lyrics and a certain amount of infidelity is taken as read but boil it down and it's all pretty wholesome, God-fearing, America-loving, red-blooded-man-loves-a-woman-nearly-as-much-as-he-loves-his-dog stuff. It's mostly maudlin but all people have patches in their lives when it helps to hear that someone else has an achy breaky ole heart too. As a country fan was quoted as saying in an *Economist* article trying to plumb the mystery of country's following in America, 'Country is the best shrink 15 bucks can buy'. Most of middle America needs a cheap shrink now and again.

We were humming along to Tom T Hall's *That's How I Got to Memphis* and that old Chuck Berry number *Memphis, Tennessee* as we rode into the town that's indelibly associated with Elvis Presley. We stayed at the Heartbreak Hotel and made the obligatory pilgrimage to Graceland, the overblown mansion that the King bought for two million dollars when he was just 22.

Elvis played the Grand Ole Opry as a teenager. They patted him on the back after his hillbilly rock set and told him not to give up his day job driving trucks. But no matter how hard or long he drove trucks it was never going to deliver him a lifestyle of the kind of demented extravagance we saw at Graceland. No expense was spared and few rules of taste or good sense observed in fitting his mansion out to the style the King imagined he ought to be accustomed. We wandered, bewildered and faintly nauseated, from room to room full of kitschy clutter: the pool room with the draped ceiling and the stained-glass light shade over the table; the white velour bedroom, its wardrobes sparkling with rhinestones and white satin on skin-tight suits; the television room with its three tellies (because the Big Guy had heard the president had three tellies). And we only saw the ground floor, as the top floor is still occupied by Presley's family.

And the fans? While we were there, a throng of them made the pilgrimage to this antebellum warehouse of Elvis memorabilia. Busloads, end on end, disgorged the disciples. Some were dressed in Elvis haute couture, some cried at his graveside. One chap had been to the mansion 12 times in the last three days. It's a cult, all right.

We crossed the state line from Tennessee into Alabama singing along to Lynyrd Skynyrd's *Sweet Home Alabama* and, in case our eyelids were drooping, a few cautionary bars of Neil Young's *Alabama*. And then of course Emmylou Harris's *Boulder to Birmingham*.

Not far from Emmylou's destination in Alabama we visited Tupelo, Mississippi, a stop on the Natchez Trace trail, and had a peek at the little wooden house in which Elvis was born in 1935. It was not unlike a miner's cottage in Granity, set among beautiful park-like lawns with a sculpture of a 13-year-old Elvis out front. We could also see the metallic blue 1949 Plymouth that took the Presley clan from here to Memphis. Needless to say, Tupelo is pretty proud of its connection to rock'n'roll royalty — while we were there the town was gearing up for the 50th anniversary of Elvis's triumphant 1956 homecoming.

And though we sang about going to *Jackson* like Johnny Cash most of the way south from Birmingham, we never did end up in Jackson, Alabama. We made a detour to Selma to see the bridge instead.

Alabama, which saw some of the worst exploitation of African Americans and most violent retributions against those seeking civil rights, is home of the spiritual. The music arose after the slave masters suppressed the animist and Muslim faiths the African slaves had brought from their homelands. As Christianity was jammed down their throats they were ordered to desist from jumping to their feet and dancing in the aisles of the churches. All musical instruments were removed.

So secret religious meetings evolved, where the slaves could speak in tongues, practise spiritual possession and express themselves in communal shouts and chants to the preacher's call. Before long, the intricate multi-part harmonies about their struggle that we know as the spirituals emerged. This strange fusion of rhythm with Christian doctrine characterised field workers' songs such as *Steal Away to Jesus* and *Swing Low, Sweet Chariot.*

Then the civil-rights movement of the 1960s fused the protest songs of Pete Seeger and Bob Dylan with soul music from the likes of Billie Holiday, Nina Simone and Aretha Franklin. The folk genres of the Appalachians and the African Americans had come together to battle the persistence of injustice.

So where did country, the most ubiquitous of the American music genres, come from? Cowboy films, it seems. Gene Autry, the yodelling cowboy, and others took the Celtic folk songs of the immigrants who settled in the east and shaped them to the aspirations of those wearing Stetsons and spurs, who nowadays drive pickups, ride Harleys and wear rawhide threads.

In Vicksburg, Mississippi, we went to a karaoke bar, a seedy joint in which the clientele was hellbent on living out something that looked for all the world like *Days of Our Lives*. Every time someone's partner so much as dared glance at another, their other half would drain their glass, bang it down on the table and flounce out into the night. Singers would spit the dummy halfway through their song when they spied their date for the evening dancing with someone else. Worst of all, everything took place to the tune — or lack thereof — of nasal renditions of dirges featuring satin sheets, tears and wasted days and wasted nights. It was all as morbid as morbid could be. Welcome to the South!

It was pretty cool listening to Janis Joplin singing the opening line to that immortal Kris Kristofferson number *Me and Bobby McGee* as we approached Baton Rouge, just as we got a kick out of singing Johnny Cash's *City of New Orleans* as we rode south alongside the Mississippi toward the Big Easy.

One of our best evenings was spent on the balcony of our hotel in Natchez with Delta blues belting out of the external speakers we carried for the iPod and watching those huge barges on which Mark Twain had once been a pilot — some of them easily 30 m long — cruising along on the river. And we accompanied the beautiful ride along the swampy gulf coast of Louisiana with the crystal clear tones of Linda Ronstadt singing *Blue Bayou*.

We sang the *Song of the South* as we rode to Texas and then moved onto Al Stewart's *On the Border* and America's *The Border* as we did the run down to Laredo, that very edgy border town that suffers an unreasonably high toll of Hispanic gangland killings. Once in Mexico we giggled along to Pat Boone's *Speedy Gonzales*. Heading back to America, the helmet karaoke numbers were Chris Cross's *Ride like the Wind*, Jim Reeves's *Adios Amigo* and Simon and Garfunkel's *El Condor Pasa (If I Could)*.

Through New Mexico and Arizona, through the desert and between all those buttes and mesas it was the cheesy falsetto and funky guitar of Russell Morris doing *Wings of an Eagle*, as the big birds soared high above us. And there were times when his lyric about losing our way in the middle of the day were just a little too close for comfort. Deserts can be monotonous enough and the baking sun mesmerising enough to make you think you've already ridden down a stretch of road earlier in the day. Sometimes you have. John Denver's *I'd Rather Be a Cowboy* certainly resonated as we entered Colorado.

The dry interior of Arizona and Utah shaded into the sagebrush and then the forested flanks of the Rocky Mountains as we approached Yellowstone. Bing Crosby singing *Teddy Bears' Picnic* was a natural choice. The plains of Idaho and Montana, rippling with wheat, cried out for the Dixie Chicks' *Wide Open Spaces*.

In backblocks Oregon we were subjected to square dancing and do-si-do. On the shores of Diamond Lake, the local dance club had organised a hoedown and the dance compere called the moves as the band played its heart out. Hundreds of women resplendent in gingham and polka dots, puffed-sleeved blouses, crinolines and pettipants swirled around their Stetson-topped, string-tied and cowboy-booted partners. Not only were the flourishes a cacophony of colour but a lesson in United States culture.

We knew we were closing on the Canadian border when we began to hear Gordon Lightfoot and Tori Amos being played in the truck stops. We were listening to *Alberta* by Eric Clapton and, soon enough, *North to Alaska* by Jimmy Horton.

On the way down the northwest through Washington state, where MoD would have had Nirvana blasting from his ear-pieces, we had Peter, Paul and Mary singing *This Land is Your Land*. As we navigated our way around the 100 m high and up to 2000-year-old redwood trees that dwell in the coastal fog belt we were reminded of our own insignificance. And as we descended to the mellow, balmy Pacific climes of the western seaboard we sang the Flower Pot Men's *Let's Go to San Francisco* and *It Never Rains in Southern California*.

Then it was time to lift the needle from the groove. This part of our world traverse was over. The last song on the playlist was Stevie Wonder's *A Place in the Sun*. We too were movin' on, movin' on.

BOILING A FROG

The Creole Nature Trail is one of the 126 Scenic Byways — stretches of highway that have been developed to show off the natural and human sights of America to their best advantage. It meanders through the swampy coastal hinterland of southern Louisiana, and disgorges the traveller at the state border with Texas.

As we neared the state line, two notable features of the landscape drew themselves to our attention. First, we could see a forest of the tall gantries of oil rigs in the distance out there in the Gulf of Mexico. And we began to see signs of the devastation wrought along this stretch of coast by Hurricane Rita in September 2005.

Every summer the southeast coast of North America cops a few hurricanes. They form over the warm waters of the Atlantic Ocean and track westward, usually hammering a few of the West Indies before striking the American mainland. The word 'hurricane' derives from the word 'huracan', which the Spanish used to describe the monster storms that kept smashing their colony in Mexico. The Gulf of Mexico provides ideal conditions for super-sizing tropical storms so Mexico, along with the gulf states of the United States, are among the hardest hit.

We had already seen the havoc Hurricane Katrina had wrought on New Orleans. The damage was done there by rain and the storm surge, which overwhelmed the flood-prevention measures that usually keep the city dry despite much of it being below sea level. Along the Texas coast the chief destroyer was wind.

It was initially feared that Rita, which boiled up into a Category 5 storm just two weeks after the destruction of New Orleans, would hit the same area. But it tracked a little to the south and had weakened to a moderately catastrophic Category 3 before it hit somewhere just between Sabine Pass, Texas, and Johnson's Bayou, Louisiana, a lightly populated area, a little after two in the morning of 24 September 2005.

Rita came loaded with winds of up to 290 km/h and literally wiped some small coastal settlements from the map. The death toll was 120 and the storm inflicted something in the order of $9 billion worth of economic damage.

As we neared where the eye of the storm had made landfall we began to see the full scale of the disaster. Here and there, on stretches of coast that looked as though they'd been scoured with a giant pot-mitt, we'd find the sand-choked outlines of streets with no buildings visible and often only a few cement blocks to show where any buildings had ever been. There were trailer homes here and there, providing temporary accommodation for the owners of the houses that had been obliterated, who either intended to build again or simply had nowhere else to go.

We saw one fellow doggedly rebuilding his house, which had been completely destroyed. Beside him, fluttering in the warm, benign breeze from the gulf, the Stars and Stripes flew gamely from a mast he had erected. It seemed to sum up so much about America and Americans. Here he was, daring to rebuild on the most hurricane-prone stretch of America's coastline with Old Glory flying over his head — the very epitome of defiance or denial, depending on your perspective.

Jo had brought along a little light reading for the trip, *The Weather Makers* by Australian ecologist Tim Flannery. It's about climate change, and what Jo had seen in New Orleans and was now seeing in Texas was fast turning her into a believer.

Gareth was an agnostic on the subject of climate change and Roger and Dave were sceptics. So what with Gareth and Roger baiting one another about faith and religion, and Roger and Dave scoffing at Jo's pronouncements of ecological doom, you can imagine our conversations along the road were seldom dull.

Like the rest of the developed world, the American economy is dependent on fossil fuels — gasoline ('petrol' in New Zealand), diesel, coal and natural gas. It's the world's largest consumer of petroleum products. The oil rigs that cluttered the skyline out in the Gulf of Mexico were helping to drag out the eight million barrels of black gold that America extracts from the ground each day. It's only the world's third largest producer of crude oil but America is by far its largest consumer. Its domestic production doesn't supply even half its consumption — America slurps its way through 20 million barrels of Texas Tea every single day.

Chemically, the fossil fuels are hydrocarbons — chains of carbon atoms combined with atoms of hydrogen and often other elements. They're organic in origin: that is, they're made up of the mortal remains of living things — plants and animals — that lived and died millions of years ago that have been lying underground subject to immense geological pressures ever since. Or at least that's the scientific explanation. You'd have to ask Roger which day of the week in 4004 BC the Lord filled the earth's gas tank.

Carbon is the basic building block of the chemicals that make up all living things — fats, proteins and carbohydrates. Plants capture carbon from the atmosphere and it is from plants that it enters the food chain. The metabolic processes of animals — by which energy is extracted from food — produce carbon dioxide as a waste product, returning the carbon that had been locked up in plant and animal matter to the atmosphere. You'll hear climate scientists talk about the 'carbon cycle' and it's this merry-go-round of carbon in the atmosphere passing through living things and back into the atmosphere that they're referring to.

Before there was life on earth there was a hell of a lot more carbon in the atmosphere than there is today. Over the millennia much of that carbon was captured by living things and taken with them to the grave, thus removing it from the carbon cycle. As Jo pointed out, waving *The Weather Makers* for emphasis, it's this carbon that's being sucked out of the ground by the oil rigs in the Gulf of Mexico, refined into gasoline, pumped into the tanks of our motorcycles, burnt in our motors and discharged into the atmosphere through our exhaust pipes as carbon monoxide and dioxide.

Her sermon set Dave off on a rant extolling the virtues of the catalytic converters on our BMWs. To listen to him, you'd almost imagine our bike riding was doing the environment a favour.

Since the level of life on earth is critically linked to the amount of carbon that's floating about, you tinker with the carbon cycle at your peril. Re-releasing carbon that has until now been languishing underground into the atmosphere will have profound effects, you can say that much for sure. It's just a matter of determining what those effects are likely to be.

While we were riding through America, Al Gore, senator, former vice president and Democrat presidential hopeful, was all over the media talking about his movie *An Inconvenient Truth*. As we watched him being interviewed by Larry King, it became clear he's fixing to make climate change a major issue in the next presidential election.

The theory is that climate change is the result of the massive release of fossilised carbon that's been going on since coal-fired steam engines were invented during the Industrial

Revolution. It's thought that the waste gases produced by burning fossil fuels — principally carbon dioxide and carbon monoxide — are major culprits. Carbon dioxide concentrations in the upper atmosphere are directly raised while carbon monoxide in the atmosphere reacts to form even greater concentrations of methane and carbon dioxide. It all conspires to become a bit like the glass roof of a greenhouse, allowing sunlight to enter but trapping within the atmosphere a proportion of the heat that is usually dissipated into space. The effect of this is the same as in a greenhouse too — the place warms up. For this reason it's often referred to as the 'greenhouse effect' or 'global warming'.

Calling it 'global warming' was a bit of a marketing mistake. Since the climate change model was first proposed in the 1980s plenty of places have experienced much colder weather than usual. We should know — our hometown of Wellington is one. This gives the sceptics an easy ride. As we shivered our way through the northerly bits of an American summer, Dave and Roger would look reproachfully at Jo.

'Where's all this global warming that's supposed to be going on, then?' they'd say.

One of the predicted effects of global warming is that extreme weather events will become more frequent and more severe, and that includes hurricanes.

The North Atlantic hurricane season of 2005 was freakishly bad however you measure it. There were 28 storms significant enough to be named. It was the first time since 1933 that the American National Oceanic and Atmospheric

Agency, which is responsible for assigning names to storms, exhausted its alphabetical list and was forced to resort to using letters from the Greek alphabet. Thirteen of these storms reached hurricane intensity, compared with the average of six. Seven reached Category 3 intensity compared with the usual two, and there were three at Category 5, though Americans have traditionally considered themselves unlucky if they've seen a single Category 5 storm in any given season.

Worse still, the 2005 season saw America hit by the most powerful Atlantic storm on record (Wilma in September), its third deadliest (Katrina in August) and its costliest (Katrina). Wilma and Rita also made the list of the 10 most costly storms, at numbers four and six respectively.

The world's weather systems, and tropical storms in particular, are generated by ocean temperatures. Areas of warm water generate hurricanes, and the warmer the water, the more intense the hurricane. It stands to reason that if the overall surface temperature of the globe rises, hurricane-prone areas will see more and more powerful storms. It also means that, as average water temperatures rise, the hurricane belt will broaden and areas that are currently immune from them will become targets. The most northerly region on America's eastern seaboard to cop hurricanes is presently Virginia. But move the northern boundary of the hurricane belt a mere 5000 km northward and you put some of the great centres of population — Washington DC, Philadelphia and New York — right in the firing line.

'Climate change is real,' Jo argued, when we talked over what we'd seen in Rita's wake that night in our digs in

Orange, Texas.

'Yes, dear,' said Gareth.

'Nah,' said Dave. 'It's just a blip. An anomaly.'

Elsewhere, while we were visiting Cuanhtémoc in the Chihuahua Desert in northern Mexico, we learned that the Mennonite population there has real problems with its water supply. The town draws its water from a deep aquifer but this has lately all but dried up. Like most of the population of Mexico — that is, those that don't take their drinking water with a dose of Coca-Cola syrup — the people supplement their supply with bottled water but that's no use for irrigation.

Just how little it rains here, and therefore how bleak the prospects were of the aquifer replenishing itself any time soon, we saw for ourselves a couple of days later when we arrived to have a peek at the Carlsbad Caverns near Alamogordo, New Mexico. We Kiwis tend to brag about the splendours of the Waitomo Caves but Carlsbad makes them look like little more than a rabbit warren. There's a dozen or so separate chambers, each with its own peculiar claim to fame. The most spectacular is the slightly prosaically named Big Room, which defies description, being 200-odd metres deep and the size of 14 football fields in area — the volume, if it means anything to anyone who hasn't been there, of six Astrodomes.

Most limestone caves are formed by rainwater made slightly acidic by the absorption of carbon dioxide, seeping through the stone and dissolving it over millions of year. This happened at Carlsbad too but the process was accelerated and augmented by the presence of oil and gas deposits in the earth deep beneath. The sulphurous fumes from the oil field percolated up through the rock and formed sulphuric acid on contact with rainwater, which was much more effective at dissolving the limestone than the usual carbonic acid.

Stalagmites and stalactites of all shapes and sizes, and the fluted columns formed when they meet, adorned the caves. Here and there we could see where a stalactite had almost but not quite descended to meet a stalagmite. We learned from the tour guide that the twain are likely never to meet, or not while there are human beings around to see them. The whole process is driven by rainfall and there just hasn't been any for the last decade. After millions of years, the dynamic process that the Carlsbad Cavern represents has stalled for lack of rain.

The lesson of Carlsbad was reinforced the following day when we rode out to White Sands, an area of the Chihuahua Desert that saw the first atomic test and is made up entirely of water-soluble gypsum sand. The fact that this vast area comprises 712 square kilometres, whole dunes and valleys of gypsum, is proof that it don't rain here much.

The Chihuahua is the largest of the so-called 'hot' deserts of North America and it's expanding as a result of higher average temperatures and lower precipitation. Not only that, but its character is changing too. Whereas its higher elevations used to be vegetated entirely in grasses adapted to the local conditions, the comparative lack of rain has meant that the hardy, woody shrubs that cover the lower reaches of the desert have begun to encroach.

'The book says that it's not just rises in temperature you have to worry about,' Jo said. 'As the sea gets warmer, the patterns of rainfall change. Some areas just won't get rain anymore.'

'Yes, dear,' said Gareth.

'So?' replied Dave the cow-cocky. 'You get some warm years, you get some wet years. Doesn't mean a thing.'

From New Mexico we rode up through Utah, Arizona and Colorado. In all three states farmers are desperate for rain. It's one of the worst droughts anyone can remember, much like the big dry afflicting outback Australia right now. Dave could be right; it could just be a particularly nasty dry spell, such as the farmers of the world all experience from time to time. But if climate scientists are right we ought not hold our breaths for the rains to come back.

For evidence that the world is getting warmer, and that the rise in temperature will have profound effects, you need only look at the cold bits of the globe.

Our ride took us along the western side of the Rocky Mountains, up to Montana, where the Glacier National Park is situated. We didn't enter the park, partly because we'd all seen the Franz Josef and Fox glaciers at home and if you've seen one jumble of icefall you've pretty much seen them all. What's more, it was hardly sightseeing weather; it was pissing with rain and we were anxious to get to day's end and get dry as quickly as possible.

The third factor in our decision to give the glaciers a miss is that there's hardly anything left of them. The area has been defrosting for more than a hundred years; the glaciers have been in full retreat since 1850, with their recession accelerating markedly in the last 25 years. This is due not only to warmer overall temperatures in the area but also to lower precipitation. Glaciers are rivers of ice that are fed from névés, basins of snow high in the mountains. In much the same way that a river will dry up if no rain falls in its catchment, glaciers halt and even shrink if no snow falls in their névé.

'Scientists use glaciers to measure climate change,' Jo said. 'If things warm up, they shrink.'

'Yes, dear,' said Gareth.

'Franz Josef was shrinking for years,' Dave replied. 'I heard it's growing again these days.'

As we rode up through British Columbia and into the Yukon, we were travelling along roads that were flanked by vast forests. But many of the trees were dead. For day after day we rode through red and russet corridors of browned forest. It looked as though it had been burnt.

Upon enquiring, we learned that a parasite, *Dendroctonus ponderosae* (the mountain pine beetle, a kind of giant borer beetle) is responsible for the destruction. The pine beetle's always been endemic to this part of North America and used to content itself with munching on old or weak trees. Its population was killed off a few times every winter as temperatures dropped below what it could tolerate, around −40 degrees Celsius.

Lately the winters have been milder, with fewer 40-belows,

and the beetle's not getting snapped in the winter. The fraction of a degree by which the climate in these parts has warmed seems to have enabled it to winter over. By the time we saw the devastating results the little critters had reached plague proportions and were laying the forest to waste. The locals we talked to reckoned you could hear them coming to settle on the trees, like a swarm of locusts.

And they're not the only organism that the comparatively mild northern winters have allowed to spread outside their usual range. From conversations with locals we learned that willow trees were advancing across Alaska's 'treeless' tundra that previously was kept that way by the permafrost.

Jo, who is from Invercargill, had prior experience of the effects of the softening of winters on promoting pests. Until recent years Southlanders never needed worry about aphids on their roses as it was just too darn cold for them to survive. Lately though, with milder winters, Invercargill rose growers have had to spray the little suckers.

If the climate does warm by its predicted 1.4–5.6 degrees Celsius over the next century, the flora and fauna of the globe will be transformed. The range of bugs such as the mountain pine beetle will be vastly extended — if the run of warmer winters that Canada has recently experienced continues the beetle may well invade the vast forests of Alberta, which account for nearly a third of the world's forest area. And while we might at last be able to ripen tomatoes in Wellington, aphids will be rampant in Invercargill.

It's not only plants and animals that will be on the move, riding on the back of climate change. Rising temperatures around the globe will broaden the range of diseases such as dengue fever and malaria.

Our climate-change sceptics were curiously quiet when confronted with the gobsmacking effects of the mountain pine beetle.

According to the global warming model, the areas of the world that will be most obviously affected are the poles. The ice caps are highly sensitive to the slightest fluctuation in temperature and it takes a rise of only a fraction of a degree to shrink the ice sheets of the Arctic and Antarctica.

There has been one potentially positive spin-off of the recent thaw of the Arctic ice sheet. The Northern Sea Route, formerly known as the Northeast Passage, from the Atlantic to the Pacific along the northern coast of Russia, has traditionally been navigable only in stages, with pack ice choking it off for much of the year. Lately though it has stayed ice-free for long enough to suggest that global warming will open a new shipping route in the near future. Likewise the Northwest Passage, which threads though the usually icebound waterways around the northern islands of Canada, seems likely to open up for commercial shipping, shaving 6500 km off the trip between Europe and the west coast of America via the Panama Canal.

In Alaska we learned that the early disintegration of the Arctic ice pack was endangering polar bears, which hunt from floe to floe. With the pack breaking up earlier and melting faster the leads of open water between floes are becoming wider — too wide for the animals to make the return trip to the safety of the main pack. The talk in the polar region is that polar bears will survive just 10 more years in the wild. But adaptation of the species is rife too and there are now grizzly/polar and brown/polar hybrids out there as nature tries to preserve the polar bear's genes.

We had a savagely cold and wet ride 570 km up the Klondike from Whitehorse to Dawson City, home of the Klondike gold rush. Halfway up the road, at a café in Carmacks, the 'gorgeous' waiter serving Jo her soup offered his armpits to her as a repository for her frozen feet, apparently an old Eskimo custom. Her disappointment was palpable when MoD pointed out the waiter was gay.

We followed more or less in the footsteps of the thousands of gold prospectors who'd climbed the Chilkoot Pass in the 1890s and caught boats down the Yukon River to its confluence with the Klondike River at Dawson City. The American novelist James A Michener has written movingly of how tough they had it, and we could sympathise. Behind the triple-glazing in our accommodation at Dawson City, we were still attempting to thaw out.

With this being the land of the midnight sun you could just about sunbathe all night. And that wasn't all there was to warm us. While we were sitting in the saloon bar of the Downtown Hotel (complete with Wild West swinging doors) we were approached by a friendly chap who asked in a pure Kiwi accent: 'Are you Gareth and Jo? And where's Dave?'

That's how we met Bill, a retired Waikato dairy farmer who was on a coach tour. He'd been following our moves on the website and reading the *Silk Riders* book. If ever you needed proof that it's a small world . . .

Dawson is hardly a city these days. It's a little town, reminiscent of Blackball on the west coast of the South Island, with a population of about 1700. It gets pretty much shut off in the winter months, which is effectively seven or eight out of 12, unless you're equipped with a sledge, a dog team and the necessary mushing skills. The streets are unpaved but there are boardwalks flanking the carriageway so you don't soil your trouser cuffs in the mud.

Back in 1898 the population of Dawson City soared to 40,000 at the height of the rush, and in all nearly 100,000 dreamers flocked to the Klondike in pursuit of 'colour' — the flecks of alluvial gold. They still come in fair numbers. The day before we arrived the local authorities had fished a prospector out of the Yukon River, where he had come to grief in search of easy wealth. Dawson was also the home of bard Robert W Service and *Call of the Wild* author Jack London; Dawsonians are very proud of that heritage.

The Yukon sports an emblem to the behaviour that has contributed to the environmental degradation of which global warming is just a part. The creeks and riverbeds around the town are criss-crossed with long, sinuous heaps of shingle. They mystified us, until we rode a little way up the pretty Bonanza Creek, site of the gold discovery in 1896 that sparked the rush. Here, abandoned in the streambed, we found the derelict No 4 gold dredge standing at the end of its trail of tailings, still parked on the spot in Claim 17 where it had gnawed away until the creek had run dry.

By 1898, once the heat had gone out of the Klondike

gold rush, large corporations began buying out individual claims and consolidating them so they could be worked by machinery such as dredges. There were 35 dredges working the Yukon in the 1890s — the shingle banks we had seen were their tailings. No 4, built in 1899, was the largest in North America. It's a mammoth machine, the size of a football field and about eight stories high. At the height of its powers it was yielding 22.7 kg of gold per day.

So far as we could tell, dredges like No 4 were the perfect polluting machines. The woodlands for miles around were cleared to feed their boilers, as they chewed the riverbed up and spat it out again in the form of muddy gravel tailings. When there was no more wood to be had locally to turn into greenhouse emissions the dredges were converted to electric power and the local streams and rivers were dammed to supply the electricity. Everything that moved was shot for the pot, and the sheer volume of noise these things produced was mind-boggling. Because precious gold flecks might stick in any stray grease in the slurry water, the engines weren't lubricated. Consequently, the bellowing of No 4 Dredge could be heard 12 km away on Dawson's Main Street.

When gold was found elsewhere the dredge was simply left where it stands today, abandoned in favour of more easily extracted lucre.

It's hard to imagine a more apt symbol of the way in which the natural environment has become a casualty in the single-minded rip, shit or bust pursuit of wealth, not just in America but right across the industrialised world. Every action has consequences and it's been a failure of the world economy since the Industrial Revolution that the cost of economic activity has not reflected the damage that has been done to the environment.

Thanks to individuals such as Al Gore and to extreme weather wake-up calls following Hurricanes Katrina and Rita, 2006 may be remembered as the year in which the Western consciousness reached a tipping point on the damage we're doing to the planet. But the message has been slow to get through, like the message that the water's becoming intolerably hot getting through to a frog being boiled. And you wouldn't necessarily believe it's getting through at all to see the way Americans live. America is the land of the automobile; everyone drives everywhere. Most of the cities we visited didn't even have footpaths because the notion that people might walk to their destinations rather than take their cars just hasn't occurred to the municipal planners. And they drive behemoth SUVs, burning gallons to the mile, cushioned from the realities of fossil fuel consumption by the low price of gasoline.

To recycling-conscious Kiwis, the disposable American society was a shock too. In the very first motel we stayed at we were bewildered by the amount of plastic and polystyrene that confronted us. The plastic cutlery and the plastic crockery was all hermetically sealed in plastic wrapping, perhaps out of concern for hygiene, but more likely for the sake of sheer give-me-convenience-or-give-me-death expediency. The volumes of rubbish an everyday activity such as eating breakfast could generate were simply appalling.

Not that we're blameless. It took Jo to point out that by buying bottled water, instead of refilling a single bottle from the tap via her water filter, we were adhering to the

175

disposable ethos. And while we tend to pick up after ourselves by instinct — and Dave goes the extra mile by cleaning up everyone else's mess at our stops as well — in a moment of carelessness one of us tossed a water bottle over a shoulder when finished (and instantly became the subject of group derision).

That was America, where there are hefty fines for littering. Across the border in Mexico no one seems to care and consequently the place is a shit hole. But that's no excuse and what we've noticed elsewhere is littering tends to abate as the standard of living rises. Perhaps it's an education thing.

Not that we can let New Zealand off the hook. We're a bit player in the global pollution business but that's beside the point. There's a hell of a lot we could do better. That Solid Energy exports New Zealand coal to China to be burnt doesn't excuse us — we're still the polluter. But most importantly New Zealand consumers could just stop buying so much stuff. All the economic research tells us that simply buying more no longer makes us any happier. We're just gluttons. Need long ago gave way to greed.

By the end of our trip Dave and Roger were pretty much convinced that global warming was a reality. Either that or they'd decided it was easier to agree with Jo. Whether she'd managed to convince them that climate change is the consequence of human activity is another matter.

In the end it boils down to this: assuming global warming is the result of human activity, it is late in the day to reverse the trend. The average surface temperature of the globe rose by 0.6 degrees Celsius over the 20th century. If the present accelerated rate of change persists it will rise by up to 5.6 degrees over the next hundred-odd years. To limit the rise to under 1 degree we would need to have cut carbon emissions by up to 80 per cent by 2050. That's a huge ask and most unlikely to occur, and the hurdle gets higher with every day that passes.

We visited a site in Utah that gave us a pretty good insight into the fate that awaits us if climate change is not reversed. At the Dinosaur National Park we saw in the cliffs the fossilised remains of 150-million-year-old dinosaurs. It's impressive and it's sobering too. Perhaps human agency has nothing to do with climate change and there's nothing to be done. Perhaps it's too late in any case. Looking at those old bones, it was instructive to remember that there had been wholesale extinctions in the history of the natural world that were due to climate change. When you're done arguing about whether or not global warming is due to human action and whether you therefore need to modify your behaviour, you should ask yourself another question.

Do you feel lucky? Well, do you, punk?

EASY RIDING

When it came to planning a motorcycle tour of North America, Gareth was torn. BMW bikes are superb and the company both at home and in Germany had treated us so well on the Silk Road that Beemers were the logical choice, especially given BMW were offering a similar partnership this time round.

But Gareth's recreational bike has always been a Harley and here we were proposing to tour the homeland of Harley-Davidson. To cruise around America on a Harley with the wind in our hair — no helmet needed — seemed like the ultimate way to go. Peter Fonda's *Easy Rider* revisited.

The dream soon foundered on consideration of the practicalities. We needed to pack enough gear for a four-month ride on the bikes — how were we going to do that if we went for the only type of Harley Gareth had ridden, the chopper-style cruiser? You can see it now: the five of us, each weighed down at the rear by luggage panniers, doing wheel-stands the length and breadth of America. Not only uncool but also downright dangerous.

Everywhere we went in America we saw Harleys, apart from in the wilds of Canada and Alaska. They're far and away the biggest-selling motorcycle in the United States and by a rough count of motorcycles on the road they have 99 per cent of the market. Even the motorcycle police we saw in Miami were riding Harley Heritage Specials.

The most popular Harley in the States though is a singularly unappealing model, which with its cowls and fairings and lights and carry-on looks like something dripping earrings when it comes up behind you. At night a glance in your rear-view mirror suggests there's a Kenworth truck on your tail, it's so well lit. These are full dressers, pricey and strictly the steed for weekend warriors.

We'd never really seen touring bikes pulling trailers before we went to America, where everyone on a Harley seems to be dragging one. We quickly worked out why. A lot of the guys who can afford these very expensive motorcycles still have to overcome the resistance of She Who Must Be Obeyed. They buy the full dresser, which comes with an intercom so backseat driving from the pillion is possible, and there's ample pillion accommodation so the, er, larger figure can mount and ride comfortably. As if the bike itself weren't enough of a compromise, there is the requirement that the make-up bag must come along too. Compromise is a two-way street so, rather than insist that the standard truckload of the stuff comes along, she'll settle for a dinky wee trailer that he won't even notice slipped in behind.

It's really a device to keep him riding sedately. At his age he should feel lucky that he's even allowed to do that!

One of these gals asked Jo what product she brings along on these trips. Chain lube was not the answer she expected.

Try hanging out through the S-bends with a trailer attached and see what happens. We did strike one poor fella who, when pulling through a corner with madam aboard and trailer in tow, didn't quite get the dynamics right and engineered a 50 m fishtail as we watched, horrified, quite convinced the bike was going to high-side them. But Harleys are heavy and, with the make-up trailer not weighing so much, the rider managed to save it all.

It's a case of 'Tow to ride, ride to tow'. The Harley trailer has brought a whole new bunch of riders into the Hell's Angels, namely the hen-pecked ageing dreamer who now has a machine to go with all the HD badges and T-shirts he's been accumulating for decades. And thanks to the moderating and accommodating presence of the trailer, his marriage has survived the purchase.

If the Harley isn't pulling the trailer it's riding on one. Many owners actually trailer their bikes to the piece of road they wish to ride or the rally they wish to attend. We met guys riding a strip of road in North Carolina who had trailered their machines down from Canada. This behaviour is very common. American riders were flabbergasted that we would ride for more than two days and dumbfounded that anyone could do more than a week.

It seems that the rationale for trailering bikes is that the owner wishes to reduce risk — self-confidence is so low that it's thought the best way to lower the odds of being killed is to reduce the amount of time you spend in the saddle.

Better to trailer the bike, ride it around the fairground and then trailer it home. And the less time the machine spends on the road, the lower the risk of stone-chip damage to the chrome, which for many is why they bought the bike in the first place.

We did meet a handful who were living — and living up to — the dream. There was 77-year-old Brad, two-up with his 72-year-old 'biker chick' wife Beryl, riding his Harley down the highway helmet-free, feeling the wind pass through where once there was hair. That's more like it. And we did come across a Harley that had been ridden hard rather than groomed and fawned over. The biker told us he rode it like a horse, on terrain no other Harley owner would attempt with him. He rarely washed it and the bike had done everything he asked of it; it had been totally reliable and a lot of fun. To the contemporary American Harley owner such treatment is tantamount to bike abuse, much as it would be to the leather and lace pretty people who now dominate the Harley customer cohort here in New Zealand. Many would rather be strung up by their tassels or stabbed to death by all the pins of their badges than see the chrome on their machine marred by a stone chip, the paintwork besmirched by dirt.

The emergence of so many converts to riding this rehabilitated American icon must be enormously satisfying and profitable for the manufacturer. For the traditional biker, however — few and far between in the United States these days — the invasion of the show ponies and promenade posers has to be the ultimate degradation of everything the bike stood for in the days of James Dean and Marlon Brando.

In Birmingham, Alabama, we paid the obligatory visit to the Barber Vintage Motorsports Museum. With more than 700 bikes and a Lotus collection to die for, as well as Porsches for miles, it's the largest bike museum in the world. It's a private facility, established by George Barber, to whom petrolheads everywhere owe a vast debt of gratitude.

We looked over the collection, which includes a Britten (number 7) and the first four-cylinder motorcycle motor, made by Fabrique Nationale (FN), a Belgian company that also made Browning machine guns.

On arrival Jo had told the guy on the desk about our trip and handed over our card — just in case that attracted special treatment. It did. We were shown right over the facility by the manager, Brian Slark. Slark said he knew only one other New Zealander, a man with whom he'd once worked on the Steve McQueen movie *The Great Escape*. That man turned out to be a boss of Jo's from long ago, namely motorbike guru Tim Gibbs of Palmerston North, who performed the fence-leaping stunt in the movie. It was a freakish coincidence.

Brian took us to the basement of the facility. Awash with chrome that gleamed under fluorescent work lights, it's the workshop in which the vintage bikes are lovingly and painstakingly restored. This side of things and the museum are George Barber's passions; the rest of the five-storey complex, with its views of the private racing circuit, hosts huge corporate functions and pays the bills. On the day of our visit, through picture windows and from the comfort of deep armchairs, we watched Porsches racing. The circuit often hosts motorcycle races too — a Superbike event had been held there a couple of weeks before.

The biker brotherhood (and sisterhood) is alive and well in America and nowhere more so than in the Northwest. All the bikers wave and at gas stations fellow riders are quick to wander across and share stories and tips on roads and campgrounds. It's a truly liberating feeling of camaraderie.

Besides the local heroes we met plenty of other grand tourists. The further north we got the more we began to meet the same people over and again. There was Geoff from Vancouver on his LC8, Al from Seattle on his 1150 Adventure, Dave from Oregon on what was quite possibly the world's lightest 1200 GS and there was Klaus (za German) on his big orange beast of a KTM.

We first met Klaus in Zion National Park, Utah, where we swapped yarns. Then he ended up camping with us in Yellowstone, Wyoming and Jasper, British Columbia. Then we ended up drinking heavily with him in Dawson and Fairbanks, Alaska, which only served to strengthen the bond further. We parted company with him in Fairbanks, but we have caught up with him since here in New Zealand as he continues his round-the-world solo route.

The further north we got, the more battered the bikes we saw became, and the taller the stories of those in the saddle. In Whitehorse MoD fell into conversation with a tall, lean man with steady, clear blue eyes who was riding a KTM 640. It turned out he was a retired fighter pilot, and the last man to have flown a Mustang under San Francisco's Golden Gate Bridge.

We were just leaving Fairbanks Honda when a chap in battered, mud-smattered oilskins chugged up on a 1980 Yamaha AG200 — a bike commonly known as 'the grasshopper' in New Zealand, where farmers use it during lambing. You won't often see them venturing off the farm and they're not even sold in the United States. Besides being a puny 200cc and a quarter of a century old, it's a two-stroke so you have to mess around mixing oil and petrol each time you fill up.

A sprightly fellow climbed off and Roger began the customary exchange of questions: where are you from, where are you headed?

The rider introduced himself as Arthur. Arthur was from Adelaide. On a whim he had shipped his farm bike to Tierra del Fuego, at the southern tip of South America, and set out for Prudhoe Bay in Alaska with nothing more specialised than a big piece of perspex wired to the front of the bike as a windshield, a pup tent and a duffel bag bungied on the back. Four months after starting out he was within striking distance of his goal — the Arctic Sea.

Roger asked what he planned to do next.

'Ship the bloody thing home again, of course,' replied Arthur in his Aussie drawl. 'Cost me five hundred nicker. Reckon I'll mount it on the wall of me lounge.'

We asked as delicately as we could and found out that Arthur was 80 years old.

'I reckoned I'd better get on and do this ride before I get too old,' he said.

To think: up to the point we met Arthur, we'd felt like rugged adventurers.

BIKED ALASKA

O ur good mate Mike O'Donnell joined us in Idaho for the northern leg of our trip, riding his 950 KTM Adventure. Shortly before he came aboard another old motorcycling buddy of ours, Pete Larson, joined in too, riding two-up with his wife Linda on a hired Harley. Pete hadn't been inducted into our corner-marking system of waiting for the following rider at forks in the road, and thus we had our moments. One of them involved a U-shaped, tree-lined lay-by where we stopped for a cup of tea. Jo rode in as the others rode out, screened from her view by the shrubs. A hell of a lot of pointless mucking about ensued, as no one had a clue who was ahead of whom and who was behind. It was all pretty funny — later, but not at the time.

Another moment involving Pete was funny at the time. The pair of us were sitting on the edge of the Grand Canyon, eating the remains of a pizza we'd brought along from our lunch stop. Helicopters such as the one we'd taken for a scenic flight over the majestic spectacle of the canyon were buzzing about, so when Pete eyed our pizza hungrily and asked where it had come from, Gareth gestured with a half-gnawed piece at one of the choppers.

'Had it delivered,' he said through a mouthful. 'They chopper it in.'

Pete eyed us, aghast. Like the rest of New Zealand, he'd heard about our windfall through the sale of our son Sam's business, TradeMe, and he clearly thought we had become conspicuous consumers on a scale at least as grand as the canyon before us. We strung him along for a while, then 'fessed up.

All of us found the Trans-Alaskan Highway, elevated as it is above the surrounding countryside and with its arrow-straight, cultured carriageway, pretty dull. But thanks to MoD's meticulous research, we were able to intersperse the boring bits with some three iconic pieces of North American motorcycling, which rivalled the Tail of the Dragon in our Appalachian traverse.

US Highway 212 from Cooke City to Red Lodge in Montana — otherwise known as the Beartooth Highway — was eventually immortalised by Robert M Pirsig's *Zen and the Art of Motorcycle Maintenance* about 40 years ago. We say 'eventually' because the book holds the dubious record of being rejected by the largest number of publishers before it went on to become a bestseller.

The Beartooth's starring role has seen bikers from across America and around the world flock here. It's rated one of America's top 10 scenic drives and one of the world's top 10 motorcycling routes. It's pretty easy to see why.

We were held up at Cooke City at the start of our traverse of the Beartooth while, somewhere up in the mountains, rugged men in check shirts used snowploughs to open the road. So it was going to be cold then — you wouldn't have known it as we cooled our heels in a balmy 25 degrees Celsius at Cooke.

Finally we got word that the road was open and were waved through. As we climbed, winding through fir forest that gradually gave way to alpine shrubs and ultimately tussock and scree, the temperature dropped markedly. We began to see patches of snow and then in some of the sheltered stretches we saw where the ploughs had been busy, with fresh snow heaped up high.

The road began to become convoluted, and we were still climbing. We caught glimpses of stunning vistas in our rearview mirrors and on the elbows of the bends. And then, as the straights opened out, Yellowstone spread out behind us and the foothills gave way to the plains of Montana ahead.

By now MoD's bike was farting and misfiring as altitude enriched the mixture; the KTM is carburetted, whereas our BMWs have fuel injection and are immune to this problem. A long stretch of the road is more than 3000 m high and we were up in the snow. We stopped at a lookout to admire the Bear's Tooth itself, a fang-like peak at the head of a valley, and shivered in the thin air. Just below us there was a lone ski lift operating and children of the well-to-do were cramming in their summer ski lessons while expectant parents looked on from the warmth of their SUVs in the carpark.

Then it was the descent, as tortuous as the climb. MoD described the road pretty well on the blog, where he said it 'resembled a huge piece of tarseal rope which has been carefully coiled, then let slip to spill down the cliff faces, all the way to Red Lodge'.

At the normally sleepy mountain town of Red Lodge, full of cafés and boutiques, Dave dived into a lingerie shop and emerged clad in a printed T-shirt. He paraded up and down the street, bringing the town to a standstill while Anita the buxom sales assistant shrieked in glee. The shirt, distinctly unfarmerlike, sported a Stars and Stripes-painted bra and suspender belt. Traffic screeched to a halt and dazed Americans demanded his autograph or, in some cases, his body. He kept most of his customers happy.

The following morning, we availed ourselves of the garage of MoD's brother-in-law, Karl Jermunson, and Dave managed to give all four BMWs a full service in less than four hours. Our luck was in when we discovered Dave.

With the exception of Gareth, who was preoccupied with portfolio management matters that day, we spent an enjoyable first part of the afternoon with the Evans family, who hosted MoD when he was in America as an AFS exchange student in 1984. Then, up the road a bit in Bozeman, Montana, we had an all-American interlude on a property belonging to Karl and another in-law, Neil Jermunson. Our hosts had laid out a buffet of handguns for the World By Bike crew to sample — we presume the NRA equivalent of afternoon tea. We started with an hors d'oeuvres of .22 calibre revolvers and automatic pistols. Our appetite whetted, we tucked into 9 mm automatic pistols, with which the team proved surprisingly accurate. Next we moved onto a lovingly tooled Smith & Wesson .357 Magnum, with which we fired wadcutters at small balloons.

We finished off with the pièce de résistance: a Ruger Blackhawk, spitting .44 Magnum lumps of lead, the favoured handgun of Harry Callahan, aka Dirty Harry.

Until you've fired a .44 Magnum you don't know the real meaning of power. The earth shakes. Small trees bend and foliage rustles with the muzzle blast and your wrists kick up over your head. As you blink, dazed in the aftermath of light and noise, you dimly perceive that whatever you were aiming at has ceased to exist.

According to MoD this is the most fun you can have with your pants on and your ammo belt hitched up.

***

We crossed into Canada at Roosville, British Columbia, and headed for Radium Hot Springs. Roger had had a bit of input into the planning of this leg of the tour, as he has kin in the area. We moved on to the beautiful Banff National Park, where we visited his brother Martyn, his wife Lois and their son Michael. The Icefields Parkway that we rode after Banff had to be one of the prettiest, most scenic stretches of road any of us had ever traversed. We stayed in a motel at a small town named Smithers; Dave managed to so charm the lady proprietor that she cried as we rode on out.

A few days later, when we arrived at Whitehorse in the Yukon, Roger's sister Judy and her husband Gordie, a local, welcomed us and filled us up with prime Canadian steaks and veges. Gordie has an interesting CV. He trained as an electrician before tossing that in to drive trucks from Whitehorse right up to Inuvik, one of the most isolated human settlements on Earth, way the hell up on Canada's Arctic Coast, keeping the Eskimo population up there in Coke and chips. He made the trip every 10 days or so while the weather permitted — much of the journey traversed frozen waterways and it wasn't possible during the two or three months of thaw.

Gordie and Judy live beside Marsh Lake, just outside Whitehorse. It's a lake for only three months a year, when the ice melts. Their boat sits idle under the snow the rest of the year awaiting the water's return. It's a totally different way of life. Like the residents of the towns and settlements further north, people endure the long, dark winter, hanging out for the couple of balmy months in summer when the sun almost never sets and they can indulge in a frenzy of outdoor activity. It's not everywhere you'll see midnight water-skiing. We'd turned in about 11.30pm each night to hear a droning outside that would increase to a roar — not a particularly large mosquito but a float plane arriving to bring in the latest batch of fun-seekers. And it's not only the people who live it up under the midnight sun — you should see the size of the vegetables they grow in Alaska.

While we were in Whitehorse, we met up with a couple of bikers, on a Pegaso and a V-Strom respectively, bikes and riders all conspicuously the worse for wear. They were returning from a visit to Prudhoe Bay on the Arctic coast of Alaska, our destination on this northerly push. They had been blessed with good weather on the northern traverse but still managed a few offs, broken spokes and bumps and bruises on the 12-hour journey. The return south, by contrast, had been turned by steady rainfall into a sticky, muddy 30-hour epic, with both riders spending as much time picking their bikes up after spills or fixing punctures as actually riding. That was food for thought as we headed for Fairbanks and our own attempt at Prudhoe.

T he ride to Dawson City was an epic; one of the coldest any of us had ever experienced. We've all taken part in the annual Brass Monkey rally in the central South Island, which is designed to make bikers feel rugged by subjecting them to ordeal by ice. But that day to Dawson made the Rangipo Desert seem like Arizona. It was sleeting the whole way and was a long, weary ride. At one stage, with no debate, we all agreed to curl up and have a half-hour sleep at the roadside.

Another iconic northern road we tackled was the Top of the World Highway, from Dawson City in the Yukon through to Tok, Alaska. Like the Beartooth, this is a summer-only road, for the obvious reason that it's deep in snow most of the year. It's not particularly high but it is so-named because from its upper reaches you feel as though you can see the world laid out at your feet — something to do with that sparkling, clear sub-Arctic air.

The road surface is gravel but it's a pretty smooth ride for the most part. Suddenly we came across the lonely border post of Poker Creek, high in the hills and manned by a single official, and then only during the summer. Small it may be but with a flourish he imprinted the largest passport stamp we've ever encountered, covering half a passport page with the outline of a moose with a full head of antlers. Then it was down the Alaska side to Chicken, permanent population 12, so named because nobody could spell Ptarmigan, a bird of the grouse family abundant in these parts. It was a long but rewarding day's ride, with the views justifying the Top of the World tag.

Everywhere we went in America we found the fraternity (and sorority) of motorcycling we'd come to expect in other parts of the world. People would approach us to ask about our bikes, ourselves and our plans and would be astonishingly generous with directions, advice and offers of assistance. Alaska was no exception, although the effete touring bikes — the Harleys and the Honda Gold Wings — had by now been winnowed out by the rigours of the roads, leaving only the rugged adventure types. And by the time we reached Fairbanks the questions had boiled down to just two: have you done Prudhoe? or, are you going all the way to Prudhoe?

Thirty years ago, BP completed the remarkable feat of engineering that is the Trans-Alaskan Pipeline from its oil installation at Prudhoe on the Arctic Coast south to the northernmost ice-free port of Valdez, British Columbia. To do it they needed first to build a road.

The Dalton Highway — 'the Haul Road' as it is universally known — is 800 km of gravel and dirt if you're lucky, or frost heave, calcium carbide grit and slushy mud if you're not. It's challenging enough without taking into consideration the 18-wheeler road trains that haunt its length.

We installed ourselves in the drab, utilitarian service town of Fairbanks, with Gareth dividing his time between the computer dealing with pressing writing commitments and

Above: *Like sands through the hourglass so are the days of our lives . . .*
Gypsum at White Sands National Park, New Mexico.

Below: *Damage to British Columbia's forests from the pine beetle.*

Above: *Move over, Big Boy!*

Below: *'Deirdre Dave' takes to the sidewalk in Red Lodge, Montana.*

Above: *Crossing the Arctic Circle — Alaska.*

Below: *Porcupine teeth make a great roadkill necklace.*

Above: *The 800 km dirt road along the Alaskan oil pipeline to the Arctic Ocean.*

Left: *Look Roger, no fear! Arctic skinny dipping.*

Left: *Moose on the loose, Alaska.*

Above: *Mud, mozzies and a perforated membrane — Alaska.*

Below: *Gareth beaten back after trying to row from Alaska to Siberia — Bering Land Bridge, Alaska.*

Left: *How's it for you,*
Dave?

Below: *Dirty girl —*
hungry, too.

Above: *C'mon and do-si-do ya pardners — square dancing, Oregon style.*

Below: *Bears' picnic.*

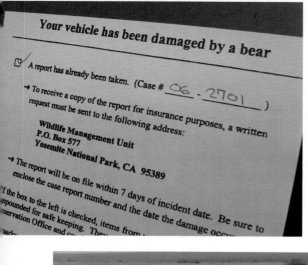

Your vehicle has been damaged by a bear

☑ A report has already been taken. (Case # 06 - 2701)

→ To receive a copy of the report for insurance purposes, a written request must be sent to the following address:

Wildlife Management Unit
P.O. Box 577
Yosemite National Park, CA 95389

→ The report will be on file within 7 days of incident date. Be sure to enclose the case report number and the date the damage occur...

f the box to the left is checked, items from ...
mpounded for safe keeping. The...
eservation Office and ...
ark...

Above and left: *What happens when bears smell food in your car . . . and the consequences — Yosemite, California.*

Below: *Death Valley parchment.*

the television, where we were keeping an eye on the weather channel.

The following day, with a thorough inspection of bikes and tyres out of the way, new brake pads fitted and loads lightened as much as possible, we hit the road for Deadhorse at Prudhoe Bay. Soon after we turned off onto the Dalton Highway we passed a sign informing us that the 911 emergency telephone number did not work north of this point. We should now rely on Channel 19 on our CB radio.

We found the road surface tolerable. It was muddy but not too bad, and there were even occasional stretches of tarseal. The trucks roaring by helped you to focus.

The pipeline kept us company the whole way. It's built on or under the ground only in a very few places, where it can rest on bedrock. For most of its span it is supported several feet in the air on insulating piles, to prevent the warm oil passing through it melting the permafrost and turning the foundations all squishy. And it's not straight — it wiggles all over the show, with the bends designed to assist it to flex without breaking under the strain of temperature changes or in an earthquake.

In what was to be an ominous precursor to his Haul Road traverse, Gareth managed to pick up a flatty pretty early on. Jo went back to him and offered to try to catch up with Dave, who was up ahead and had the puncture gear. Off she roared. Dave had done the right thing and had stopped after he'd failed to see the reassuring sight of Jo's headlight in his rear-view mirror. He waited until he saw a headlight approaching. Once he saw her coming, he assumed all was well and took off. Jo tried vainly to catch him for a while, then gave it up and went back to wait with Gareth. Unfortunately, such was the visibility that Dave had set off while Jo was still a long way astern and put in a good few miles before he realised what the situation was. Damn all that sparkling, clear sub-Arctic air!

***

The truly unexpected aspect of the Dalton Highway was its beauty. MoD reckoned it reminded him of the road between Haast and the Gates of Haast in Westland but on a grander scale.

We stopped for photographs at Milepost 115, where there is a sign marking the Arctic Circle. We had to queue, as this is where your American weekend warrior flogs his Jeep Cherokee to get a photo of himself beside a certifiable hard-man landmark. It was warm, easily 25 degrees Celsius, which was not what we expected just a few hundred kilometres short of the Arctic Ocean. Our first day's ride ended at Milepost 175 in desolate little Coldfoot (population 13). Staying the night in the prefabs of this camp erected to house workers who built the pipeline back in the 1970s, we basked in the comparatively safe atmosphere of the shelter, insulated from the harsh outdoors, and read a bit about the pipeline in the literature lying around. Like the day in 2001 when local troublemaker Daniel Carson Lewis shot a hole through a weld in the pipe and 250,000 gallons of oil spilled. For that moment of madness he's serving 10 years in the clink. Though the rooms were basic and far from soundproof they were comfortable and sure beat a tent in environs where the bears are pretty mean. And the food at the mess was big, bulky and welcome.

Coldfoot contained a real surprise for us — a fabulously appointed visitor centre that each night ran lectures on aspects of the local environment. Every visitor to town attends as there is no other show on, and it's well worth it. We were treated to a lecture by a young Athabascan Indian woman who covered all aspects of growing up in the isolated fish camps. Though their population was depleted compared with decades ago, it was encouraging to hear her say how the younger ones were increasingly returning to their traditional homes and simple lives, as the lustre of modern urban life wore thin.

Shortly after departing the following day, we passed the 'last tree' on the highway at Milepost 235 and climbed up to the Atigun Pass, high in the Brooks Range, where the countryside had begun to look more like the Himalayas. Over the pass and down the last north-facing slope before the Arctic Ocean, the landscape changed from alpine to distinctly arctic, with tundra taking over. It was vivid green — like the residents of these northern latitudes, the vegetation lives it up in the short growing season — and interspersed with slate lakes. And it began to cool noticeably as we descended. By the time we reached Deadhorse, the end of the Haul Road, it was a decidedly fresh 3 degrees Celsius.

Just short of our destination Gareth's puncture played up again. Whether it was a new one or the same one returning we couldn't tell but it was damned inconvenient, happening so tantalisingly close to the end of the run north. The tyre decided not to cooperate and wouldn't sit back on the rim properly. Luckily, back in Fairbanks while we were packing for the Haul Road, MoD had seen Jo umming and aahing about packing the $6 compressor she had picked up along the way. We carry little bottles of CO_2 for emergency tyre re-inflation, and she wondered aloud whether these would be enough or would the compressor just be redundant extra weight. MoD assured her it would be a useful piece of extra equipment. So it proved. Jo managed to get the pressure of Gareth's tyre back up to 90 psi and, while he had to ride with a wobble for the last remaining miles, at least he got there.

When we finally stood among the oil wells we were elated. We'd made it without a single off and only a few punctures to liven things up. We managed to photograph a dead horse lying in the tundra just on the outskirts of Deadhorse — put there, perhaps, by the local tourism office. If so, it was about the only facility they'd bothered to install. There weren't even any signposts among the cluster of what looked like refrigerated shipping containers that comprised the town. It took us an age to find our accommodation, a bunch of containers called the Arctic Caribou Inn.

Not that we were content to stop at Deadhorse. The Arctic Ocean beckoned, another seven miles down the road, and we joined a tour group heading there — the only way we could go given the oil company jealously guarded access to its installation. The tour guide was packing a .44 Magnum on his hip, and the safety briefing we received largely featured polar bears. On our arrival at the shores of the Beaufort Sea, we got another briefing on polar bears. Then we alighted from the bus and walked out onto the slate-grey shingle strand that passes for an Arctic beach and, as the other tourists looked on aghast, we stripped down to our swimmers and dived in. MoD had brought along a cigar and an ounce of whisky, entertaining visions of sitting up to his hips in the Arctic puffing on a stogie and warming himself with a dram. That dream died an icy and early death in the deathly cold water. And being first on video duty in the freezing air, Jo was a little too chilled for full immersion when her turn came. A little dip up to her knockers sufficed. We emerged, gasping and got an even ruder shock: down the beach towards us, buck naked, swinging his hips lasciviously and waving a New Zealand flag over his head, came Dave Wallace. Now that's style.

That evening Jo was wandering around with her camera in the midnight sun outside the converted shipping containers that comprised our accommodation when a huge pickup pulled in. A great, bearded bear of a man jumped out and did a double-take at her.

'I've met you somewhere before,' he said in a Texan drawl, his bushy eyebrows knitted.

'Oh, yeah,' she said. 'And how long have you had out here to dream up a pick-up line like that?'

'No, no. I get choppered in, three weeks in, three weeks out,' he said. 'I'm right. Seriously. I've met you before. You were doing the Dragon. I was on a Harley.'

You and a hundred others, she thought. But then he showed her a photograph of his green machine at Deal's Gap and the nickel dropped. It was big Bubba. He's a welder and, as he'd told Jo when they'd first met, a damn good one at that. He's much in demand at Prudhoe, where everyone's pretty anxious that the quality of the welding on the oil pipelines is all it can be.

North America's a big continent but it's a small world.

I t was yet another shock the following day to emerge from the triple-glazed, air-conditioned comfort of our accommodation into the crisp, Arctic air. We had to muck about finding petrol facilities — not hard, you wouldn't have thought, in an area that produces eight per cent of America's oil — and eventually located a hand-operated bowser with which you drew petrol from a drum. Then we had to track down a workshop that could reseat Gareth's back tyre on its rim, where the bead had settled out of place after the last of his previous day's punctures. After all that was attended to we headed out on the return trip.

It was pretty uneventful until just before we got back to the Atigun Pass, where Gareth heard the all-too familiar whup-whup of a puncture. So we had yet another tea-drinking, tube-changing party at the roadside, netting deployed to save ourselves from the plagues of mosquitos that seem to do all right in the Arctic regions. A versatile sari-like item of apparel that Jo takes everywhere proved ideal for keeping the disassembled wheel parts clean. We later learned that the CB airwaves the truckies use to keep in touch were alive with reports of our predicament and our whereabouts so a rig coming over the crest of the hill didn't collect us.

We overnighted in Coldfoot again, listening apprehensively to the rain drumming all night on the roof. While there we learned that two other bikers had had far less luck. One had been airlifted out after a pretty nasty encounter with a stone that had been flung up by a passing truck and had hit him chest-high with almost as much force as a Jerry Collins spot tackle. The other had run his main bearing and was waiting glumly for a truck to take his bike the rest of the way on a pallet. We weren't without problems either — to Gareth's recurring puncture tribulations, Jo added burst fork seals which compromised her front-end stability.

We quickly found that the rain had altered everything about the Haul Road when we set out the next day. The greatest challenge was visibility. As the road trains roared by on the wet road they would shower us with shit. Wiping it from our visors merely turned the splatter into an impenetrable smear so we found ourselves having to stop to give them a decent wash.

Eventually this got too much for us. When we came across a truck stopped at road works somewhere south of Coldfoot, we pushed in front of him and idled our bikes, awaiting the all clear. When it came it was like dropping the flag to start a race. We were off, the truck roaring and whistling through its gears in our wake.

The trucks in America don't behave quite like the lumbering, underpowered trucks in Kiwiland. They're huge, with power units to match, quite capable of cruising along at America's elevated highway speeds. What's more, with 18 wheels on the road, they have a little more traction than a biker wobbling along the rutted mud and grit roadway with his knobblies all gunked up. Shortly after we thought we'd left it for dead, the great bluff front of the thing loomed in Dave's rear-vision mirror. Discretion being the better part of valour, Dave took the first opportunity that arose to let him through.

Jo was next and she too pulled off as soon as she could, though she nearly lost it in the windrows at the roadside. The monster then hunted down Roger, who made a bit of a race of it, darting nervous glances at the grille filling his rear-view mirror, before it passed him. As soon as Gareth saw it overtake Roger he pulled into a lay-by. As he sat there, Roger appeared, applied his brakes and locked up, shooting forward in the liquid mud toward Gareth, threatening to T-bone him. Fortunately Gareth had seen what was about to happen and heard Roger's warning shouts. He was able to let his clutch out and get out of the way just in time.

Meanwhile, in a scene reminiscent of that 1980s Steven Spielberg film *Duel*, in which a crazed truckie chases Denis Weaver across the desert, the rig was closing on MoD. MoD was determined to keep in the clear ahead of it so he gave it a run for its money.

The battle evolved into a genuinely dangerous situation, with MoD riding faster than the con-ditions permitted him to do safely and the truck right up his backside, giving him no room for error. Eventually, dejected that commonsense had to score one over his competitive instincts, he pulled aside and let it pass. When we came across him he was quite shaken by the experience.

The sensible thing, of course, would have been to let the truck go first from the start.

We hauled into Fairbanks that night tired but exhilarated. The weather gods had smiled on us and we'd accomplished our mission with no serious mishaps. We could hardly recognise one another or our bikes under the thick dun-coloured mud we wore, but that was nothing a shower, an industrial-strength washing machine and a water blaster couldn't fix.

As she was lubricating the chain of her bike at our motel in Fairbanks, Jo was approached by two blokes who were intrigued to know where she'd been to get into such a state.

'Prudhoe,' she told them.

They looked a little downcast at that. They told her they'd just called off their own long-planned assault on the Haul Road after hearing the horror stories about the ride.

'Now we're just gonna have to do it,' one of them said. 'We can't let a girl do it while we skulk off and run, can we?'

She smiled and retorted, 'I'm not just a girl. I'm a granny too.'

They mooched off, not realising that they'd probably faced the most dangerous moment of their tour right there.

Being back in Fairbanks was a significant milestone in other ways. Here we parted company with MoD, who headed south quickly to rendezvous with the rest of his family on holiday in Vancouver. And Roger took time out as well to return to Whitehorse and spend more time with his sister. We would connect with him again on the ferry heading south through the Inner Passage to Vancouver Island. The two of us and Dave took off for the airborne excursion to Nome, a mere 900 km west, where no roads ventured.

DUBYALAND

The town of Vicksburg, Mississippi, was the scene of one of the decisive battles of the Civil War. For six desperate weeks in 1863, Union general Ulysses S Grant laid siege to a strong force of Confederate forces under the command of John C Pemberton. It ended on 4 July, with Pemberton's surrender and the decision — uncharacteristically humane in this vicious little spat — to allow the 30,000-strong Confederate army to go free upon their word that they would not take up arms in the war again. Apparently it wasn't until after World War II — more than 80 years later — that the good folk of Vicksburg could bring themselves to celebrate Independence Day. Seems it just didn't feel right to make merry on the anniversary of the town's darkest hour.

We rolled in fresh from our visit to the Selma Bridge and deeply impressed by the civil rights movement. We quickly worked out there weren't too many Vicksburgers we wanted to share these thoughts with. It's not exactly a hotbed of liberalism and tolerance. Jo spoke to several of the locals and they were all proud to call themselves 'rednecks', even if they couldn't quite come up with a consistent definition of the term.

We booked into a place called the Battlefields Inn and settled into the bar for a steak and a drink. It was full of rednecks. Later in the evening, once the local jazzman had got into his groove, a redneck approached Jo and took her for a very formal turn around the dance floor. It was the fulfilment of one of her lifelong ambitions.

When you look at how the states voted in the last two presidential elections, what you see is a big red map of America with blue edges, where red states voted Republican and blue states voted Democrat. It's as though a deeply conservative country has been soaking in liberalism only long enough to absorb it at its very edges, the wishy-washy, namby-pamby, bleeding-heart liberal centres of urban population on the east and west coasts.

One of Gareth's primary motivations in plotting our course through 'backblocks' or 'heartland' America was to try to find out for himself what the hell George W Bush was doing in the White House. For Americans to have elected him once seemed unfortunate but to have re-elected him looked like a gross dereliction of the nation's democratic duty. Our itinerary was thus constructed to take us through the middle of the red bits on the electoral map — through towns like Vicksburg.

We got talking to a bunch of local bikers who were drinking in the Battlefields Inn. They were wearing the ubiquitous tasselled jackets of Harley-Davidson riders and Harley badges to boot. They were mostly armed services veterans who between them had seen action in Vietnam, the first Gulf War, Afghanistan and the latest Gulf War in Iraq. They ranged in rank from private to no less than a retired general. One of them was back home for limited time, between tours of duty in Iraq.

It was inevitable we'd get yarning to them about American foreign policy in general and the Iraq War in particular.

None of them thought the war was a great idea but try as we might we couldn't seem to crack a joke about it that hit the right note. Our attempts at making light of it kept snagging on an underlying tension. You might get them to accept that the war had been misconceived from the outset and that it had been badly managed since but we were left in no doubt that you still had to respect the men and women putting life and limb on the line.

We soon realised that New Zealanders have all but lost a sense of what it's like to have their young people overseas getting wounded and maimed. That's why most heartland Americans (as it seemed to us, staring at the tailgates of their pickups) could slap a bumper sticker on their vehicle reading 'Support our Troops' with a perfectly clear conscience, no matter how disinterested they were in the rights and wrongs of the war, and never mind if they were actually, deep-down, truth-be-told opposed to it. Most of all you didn't want to go around crowing: 'It's Vietnam all over again!' Those present who'd served in Vietnam proved extremely touchy about that whole business. Again, it pays to remember that ordinary Americans suffered terribly there, and it wasn't just their national pride that was hurt. Many died, many were wounded and so many more were psychologically scarred. They returned to their homeland and found that they didn't quite fit in and, in the way of misfits everywhere, many soon became bikers.

Nowadays that hatchet has well and truly been buried. Where you stood on Vietnam is no longer relevant but all Americans concur that the soldiers — remember that in those days they were conscripted — made huge sacrifices. Americans are dead set on avoiding any repetition of the disgraceful treatment they dished out to their Vietnam vets with those serving in Iraq. No matter what goes on over there, as far as the American public is concerned all in Iraq are heroes.

Nor do you want to blame the president for the mess America's in. We found this just about everywhere we went. It was one thing to speak up against the war. But if we took that criticism to what appears to the rest of the world to be its logical conclusion and laid the blame at the door of the Oval Office, we were told in no uncertain terms that we had overstepped the mark. It's part of the rabid patriotism that prevails in America, where Old Glory flutters in front of a good proportion of the houses. You're brought up revering the flag and the office of president in equal measure. Merely by being elected, George W Bush was transformed from a dim-witted, gauche frat boy into one of history's chosen elite — a member of the club of American presidents that are royalty no matter what the quality of their policy is. That he's presiding over one of the biggest foreign policy cock-ups in his nation's history is, for heartland Americans, beside the point.

What's more, the longer we debated the issue, the more we got the sense that our American companions felt we weren't really qualified to express a view, given we were from a small, lucky country that didn't literally (as they saw it) carry the weight of the world on its shoulders in the way America did. Further, from those who knew a bit about New Zealand, the view was that we are selective moralists, nuclear-free evangelists because we can afford to be but as duplicitous as anyone should the occasion arise. We were reminded a couple of times of David Lange's about-face over the imprisonment of the French *Rainbow Warrior* saboteurs when we were threatened with an end to our butter trade.

And it wasn't just in Vicksburg that we encountered the notion that we were unqualified to comment. We met plenty of people from one coast of America to the other who were prepared to tell us that it was the burden of the US of A to be the world's policeman, whose sacred mission was to shine the light of freedom and democracy into the dark corners of the world. It was an added burden, we were given to believe, to have poxy little countries like New Zealand freeriding on all the wholesome order and discipline America brought to a messed-up globe.

We had a look around Vicksburg the following day. It was a pretty town that made a feature of the National Military Park commemorating the 1863 siege. There were cannons and monuments everywhere, a monument for the fallen of each state, Union and Confederate alike. There were the restored remains of an ironclad gunboat and a bunch of caves in which the townspeople and Johnny Rebel forces took shelter from the withering bombardment by the Unionists.

There were also restored remnants of the fortifications both sides used during the siege. They were unbelievably close together. You tend to forget how intimate warfare was in the days before effective artillery and air power. The sides were separated by little more than a hundred paces of grassy field. Of the estimated 19,000 soldiers — 10,000 Union and 9000 Confederate — interred in the fields around Vicksburg, 13,000 were never identified.

On our tour through heartland America we couldn't help but notice that there were fresh wreaths in many of the graveyards. We hadn't seen so many fresh wreaths since our trip through war-torn Bosnia the year before. It seemed it was the backblocks of America that were bearing the brunt of Bush's adventures in blunderland.

The day before we were to return to Fairbanks from Nome, Jo met a young Eskimo man dressed in desert fatigues, and asked where he was heading so early on a Sunday morning along the otherwise abandoned dirt streets.

'To Iraq, ma'am,' he replied.

Along with the other volunteers of the Alaskan Division, he had been called up and was really excited to be off on such a huge adventure. He'd never been away from the Bering Sea coastline and indeed seldom far from the fish camp where his family lived, clinging on to that coastline.

'I'm off to see the world,' he said to her and beamed — the same grin worn by every young man who ever went to war.

Ignorance, as they say, is bliss. All the way back east we pondered what a hell of a way *that* was to escape the traditional lifestyle of his people. Swapping the Bering Sea for the battlefields of Basra didn't seem that much of a step forward to us.

It came as some surprise that wherever we went we found Americans who really, truly believed they were at war. Partly it was this mood that inflamed their natural patriotism, and diluted whatever capacity they might otherwise have had for judging the quality of their administration.

On our way to the Amish community we found an unassuming signpost at the side of the road in Somerset County, rural Pennsylvania, directing us off into a field backed by a stand of trees and a low hill. We bumped our way down a track to a temporary memorial, festooned with wreaths and flags, to the 40 passengers and crew of United Airlines Flight 93, the only one of the four airliners hijacked on 11 September 2001 that didn't reach its target. Once they realised their plane had been hijacked, those aboard called people on the ground by cellphone, whereupon they learned what had happened at the World Trade Center only a few minutes earlier. Knowing they were facing certain death, a group of passengers — including a New Zealander — decided to try to stop their plane reaching whatever destination its hijackers had planned. They succeeded in overpowering the terrorists, or at least in forcing them to abort their mission and nosedive the Boeing 737 into that field in Pennsylvania.

The site was on private land. We met the bloke who owned it, who was there the day the plane went down. It was a huge explosion, he said. The trees caught alight in the resulting fireball. As he talked about it on that chilly afternoon we could see the emotion in his face. We could see in his eyes that no matter how many times he told his story he would never really get over that September morning.

Even those Americans with no first-hand experience of the events of 9/11 were deeply shocked by it, far more so than the millions of viewers of other nationalities who witnessed them on television. It's not hard to understand how it created a constituency for Bush's foreign adventures in Afghanistan and Iraq. To your average American, someone had attacked America and they badly needed attacking right back.

The September 11 atrocity tapped something deeply engrained in the American psyche. We quickly learned that the population of the Home of the Brave is scared shitless most of the time. While the Vicksburg boys were looking over our bikes, they noticed Jo's topbag, which still had the map of the Silk Road on it. They were gobsmacked by the distances we'd covered on that trip and intended to cover on this tour. They took photographs and shook their heads and pointed at us as though we were a freak show.

But when they saw that the wiggly line of our route through Central Asia passed through Iran, they were literally speechless. They just could not believe that decent, God-fearing, Western people would go there.

That was understandable. The rhetoric between the

United States and Iran has been pretty salty over recent years and these days, with Iran labelling the States 'the great Satan' and the States leading the charge to prevent the mullahs getting their hands on nuclear weapons, Americans can be forgiven for thinking they wouldn't be that welcome over there.

But their reaction when they learned that we were shortly off to Mexico was more surprising. A couple of them took Dave, Roger and Gareth aside to have a go at them for daring to expose Jo to Mexican border protocols, which they happened to know for a fact routinely involved raping women. They were serious! And they rebuked the boys when they refused to see reason. As far as they were concerned we were just too irresponsible for words.

It's fear — the fairly typical American tendency to make mountains out of molehills. We struck it elsewhere too. We made a detour in Florida to visit a former neighbour of ours, a nice bloke named Arnie who had lived near us in Oriental Bay for a few years with his family and worked for Telecom. Unlike the vast majority of Americans, he was a pretty well-travelled fellow. But when we were talking to him on his home turf in Florida he told us he was afraid to travel these days. He folded his arms across his chest and shook his head and vowed that he would never set foot outside the United States again.

The dedicated consumer of CNN, full of images of the smoking rubble of United States embassies around the world and hooded American citizens in orange boilersuits kneeling before AK47-toting terrorists, would quite understandably think twice about going abroad waving the Stars and Stripes and flashing their United States passport.

But it's not just fear of the outside world. In Utah a big hairy bloke approached Gareth in the forecourt of a gas station and was looking over his bike enviously. He asked what our plans were. Gareth told him we were touring North America.

The man blanched.

'You're not going to Colorado, are you?'

'Yep,' Gareth replied.

'No, man,' the big fella said, wagging his head. 'You can't ride in Colorado. The drivers are mad over there. They'll knock you off your bike. They do it all the time.'

'Oh, yeah?' Gareth replied, a little sceptical. 'So where do you live then?'

'Denver. That's how I know. My lady won't let me own a bike since we shifted to Colorado.'

※※※※※※

It's fear and it stems from the other striking characteristic of heartland Americans, their insularity.

We went to the States prepared for most Americans to have little or no idea where New Zealand was. We took along the same inflatable globe we'd used on the Silk Road to show people and it got plenty of outings in the United States.

The most memorable response we got when we answered the question 'Where you folks from?' was from Randy Gums, that gloriously named resident of a small town high in the Appalachians.

'Noo Zealand?' he echoed, and screwed up his stubbly,

buck-toothed face. 'I hate Germans!'

But contrary to the jingoism we tend to associate with Americans, the common response in those sorts of places, once we'd put them straight on New Zealand's lack of proximity to Germany, was: 'Why in hell you wanna come all the way to a shit hole like this?'

It was no surprise that most Americans we talked to didn't have much of a clue about the world outside America. What we quickly noticed though was that few Americans in the backblocks had more than the foggiest notion about anything over their state line. More than once, when we asked someone whether they were local, the conversation would go something like this:

'I'm from here, but my husband ain't. He's not from round these parts at all.'

'Oh? Where's he from?'

'Oh, he's from such-and-such.'

'Where's that?'

'Across the line. Next state.'

In many cases the town in question in the next state would be a matter of kilometres away. Most Americans aren't that mobile. Before we saw for ourselves the isolation in which they lived, reminiscent of accounts of village life in medieval Europe, we might have scoffed at stories of people who lived and died in modern America without ever having seen the sea. But it's easy to believe. Like our biking pals in Vicksburg, people were just blown away by the map of our intended route on our panniers.

'You're going all the way to Alaska?' someone in New Mexico would gasp.

'Yes, but it's all part of a bike trip round the world,' we'd reply.

'Sure, but you're going to *Alaska?* On bikes?'

I don't think any of us had quite expected to be the *cause célèbre* that we'd been in Central Asia when we rode into towns in America. But we came close. At one stage we were stopped alongside a school bus, the standard-issue, *Forrest Gump*, yellow affair. While Gareth yarned with the driver, Jo passed little bookmarks featuring a photo of the bikes in the desert on the Silk Road she'd had printed up to the kids who were hanging out the windows. We went our separate ways but that evening Gareth received an email from the bus driver, who'd clearly got our details from one of the bookmarks. He thanked us for making their day — we were the most exciting thing to have happened in their lives for months. We'd had many such heart-warming moments on the Silk Road, but hadn't quite expected it in America.

We were a real novelty too in places like Randy and Fanny Gums's hometown when we hauled in, four of us dressed in spacesuits astride these exotic machines. It wasn't unlike riding into villages in Serbia or Turkmenistan — yet here we were in the heart of the high-tech US of A. Consequently, when Gareth lost his keys in that town it wouldn't have been hard for the locals to work out whose they were. You can picture the conversation as they scratched their heads over them.

'Well, they sure's heck ain't the keys for Randy's pickup.'

Fortunately, Gareth had a spare set, otherwise we'd have been stuffed. Needless to say, you oughtn't hold your breath looking for the Appalachians BMW dealership, and without a BMW dealer there's no way to start the bikes without their own key, each of which contains a unique electronic chip.

Meanwhile, the problem confronting the locals of Gumsville was getting in touch with us. They had our email address — if only they could use email. Happily, there was a girl in town who knew a bit about it and, using the local drug store's computer, she was able to contact us. Gareth got her to send the keys to MoD's relations in Montana and sent her a copy of the *Silk Riders* book to thank her.

I n a nation where even the major newspapers in each state feature just one or two pages of out-of-state news, the spectacular insularity of the majority of the population is understandable. Stock, stockfeed and fertiliser prices, local weather and local sport are about all they need to know. And the big political issues are where the candidate stands on abortion and perverts. Iraq? Thank the Lord America can save the world!

T he fearfulness of Americans and the abject terror they felt in the wake of 9/11 account for George W Bush's re-election. He was, so far as the heartland electorate could tell, the only candidate willing, able and foolish enough to deal to whoever the hell had done this terrible thing.

All very understandable so far. But it's far more unsettling to consider how Bush got there in the first place. Gareth was able to enlighten us on this, from John Micklethwait and Adrian Wooldridge's *The Right Nation*. This studied the rise of the Republican Party since its low point in the 1960s, and its authors concluded that you couldn't really account for American conservatism in the same terms as you could account for political movements in a British or European context. Americans are different. And one of the ways in which they're different is they consider themselves to be different from the rest of the world. Micklethwait and Wooldridge call this 'exceptionalism' — the unshakable American conviction that America is exceptional in world terms. It's more godly, more democratic, more free, more rich and just generally more apple pie and cream than anywhere else on Earth.

You can partly attribute this to the religious fundamentalism that's the backbone of American conservatism. It's the belief that America is God's chosen country, formed by people who fled the old, corrupt and mostly Catholic order of Europe to form the New World. Protestantism has always regarded the work ethic as among the greatest of all human virtues so American Protestants see the material success of America, its booming economy, as evidence of God's favour. And as the Cold War was always sold as a battle of good (Christian, free, democratic) against evil (communist, unfree, despotic), the collapse of the Soviet Union was seen as the Lord's verdict on the competing systems. The evil empire was wrong; America was right and therefore vindicated.

Even those who are not particularly motivated by religious fundamentalism can believe in the 'manifest destiny' of America as the world's leader in the ideals of constitutional democracy, human rights, personal freedom and the rule of law. For these folk America is above the standards it sets for the rest of the world precisely *because* it sets the standards. This is what accounts for the peculiar American ability to compartmentalise and to live according to some quite glaring double standards. Americans kill and die for principles such as the rule of law — and yet they're almost unanimously behind the Bush administration's treatment of 'terror suspects' who are arrested, detained without charge or trial and probably even tortured at 'black sites' around the world and at Guantanamo Bay. To call this a double standard is to be kind.

Let's take another example. Americans are staunch proponents of the freedom of the market at home yet America is one of the greatest obstacles there is to free world trade, with the vast majority of its farmers, hopelessly uneconomic as their operations are, propped up by massive subsidies and tariff regimes. And a third example: as far as America is concerned, the United Nations and the International Court of Justice are great for the rest of the world but needn't apply to the world's first citizen, America. Rules are for the guidance of wise men but for the regulation of fools.

It was preaching and practising this doctrine of 'exceptionalism' that enabled Ronald Reagan to complete the comeback of Republicanism from the nadir of the 1960s, and that enabled Reagan's vice president, George Bush Sr, to consolidate the Grand Old Party's hold on power in the 1980s. That period of Republican rule so clearly demonstrated where the hearts and minds of hick America lay that it exerted an irresistible gravitational pull on the Democratic Party. Clinton's presidency was notable more for its 'Republican-lite' flavour than it was for any opposition to what the Republican Party stood for. If anything, the Clinton presidency was the most worrying sign of all, as it proved that the election of George W Bush was no aberration. The American electorate was merely waiting for a credible Republican candidate. Clinton had simply filled a gap. For all his celebrated cerebral challenges, George Dubya was shrewd enough to pepper his proposed administration with key personnel from his dad's days in power. That way, after the moral embarrassments of the Clinton years, American voters felt they knew what they were getting when they voted for the later-model Bush.

***

In New Orleans Gareth enjoyed locking horns on the subject of politics with an expatriate New Zealander who has, since shifting to America, become more American than the Americans. This bloke represented what you might call the 'college' end of the spectrum of Republican support, consisting of relatively well-educated, middle-class conservatives. He was a living, breathing preacher of American exceptionalism, who believed that neither America nor its president could do any wrong, simply by definition. He acknowledged that there was criticism from the rest of the world of the American way of life but believed it could only be attributed to envy.

His smugness made Gareth appreciate that this 'no matter what' idolatry of the United States threatened any hope of seeing objective, even-handed analysis emanating from that society in the near future.

America *is* exceptional because for everyone in the world

to have the same standard of living as the average American we'd need seven globes' worth of resources. Not that everyone wants to live like an American. Indeed, everyone needs Americans to live differently — to tread a little more lightly on the earth.

From what we saw there's a long way to go before America gets around to seeing it that way. Its political economy is just not that adroit.

Gareth and his New Orleans sparring partner parted amicably enough. But while one went on his way thinking 'God bless America', the other saddled up and rode off thinking 'God help us all'.

GIVING IT DEATH

From Port Hardy, where the Inner Passage Highway ferry discharged us on the top of Vancouver Island, the highway is not unlike the road from Tokoroa to Atiamuri, so long as you multiply the length by 10. It's all forest-covered rocky outcrops interspersed with some nice rivers. The island is the summer playground for Canadians who live inland, and in the heat of mid-July the crowds were certainly there. It was pretty but not a patch on the wilderness of Alaska.

We spent the night in Vancouver, where Jo found a cousin, Steve Elder, and set about catching up. It turns out that emptying his beer fridge, enjoying a feed off his barbecue and fitting in a few words between mouthfuls is the best way to catch up with someone after 30 years. Vancouver reminded us of Wellington: very vibrant, with a cosmopolitan feel to it. We loved it and the weather was balmy and clear.

Then we hit the road for what was to be the home straight,

the long run down the western seaboard. In Seattle, we dined with John Maclean and Leyette and Paul Callister, yet more members of the great Kiwi diaspora. They had emailed and urged us to stay on our way through. They opened their home on the shores of Union Lake to us, laying on a fine Kiwi-style barbecue after first taking us on a great kayak trip around the lake to see the sights, including the houseboat that featured in the sugary Tom Hanks movie *Sleepless in Seattle*. It wasn't quite as relaxed an outing as you'd imagine — with float planes coming and going every few minutes we had to keep our wits about us.

Jo had her troublesome front fork seals fixed in Seattle. The calcium carbide grit they spread on the Alaskan roads liquefies and then recrystallises on the shafts of your forks and, if you're slack about chipping it off, it rips the shit out of the seals as the shafts slide up and down when you bounce over the bumps. Failure of these seals is a bit like having worn shock absorbers in a car, and you get that wobbly feeling in your shoulders and in the pit of your stomach.

The BMW bike shop was slick, efficient and pricey. They serviced the bike as well. It wasn't until she was a few hundred kilometres down the road that Jo gave her chain a nudge with her toe, as she's accustomed to do to check its tension. There wasn't an iota of movement there, despite the big bold label that the manufacturer puts adjacent to the adjustment screws warning against over-tightening. It wasn't the first time Jo's been grateful for her wary, mistrustful nature and her refusal to assume the job's been done properly. If she hadn't checked and the chain had broken — and odds on it would have before we'd got much further — she'd have put it all down to bad luck.

We rode down through the magnificent redwood forests of lower Washington state and Oregon, and then joined the Californian coast road. The weather got warmer as we went south and by the time we were in the vicinity of San Francisco it was stinking hot — 115 degrees in the local money (46 degrees Celsius). If you left your visor up for more than a few minutes you'd be contemplating your tomato complexion in the mirror for days afterwards, before the peel set in.

We arrived at a vantage point at San Francisco Bay and saw, well, nothing, apart from the very top of the pylons of the Golden Gate Bridge protruding from the fog that filled the bay like a bowl.

About 20 km before the bridge, Jo had her worst moment of the trip. She was in the fourth of five lanes and travelling about 120 km/h when she heard a 'bang' and her bike got the wobbles. Riding a straight line at these speeds on a flat rear tyre is hard enough; getting across four lanes of traffic like that is pretty dicey indeed.

She got across, greatly assisted by the courtesy of Frisco drivers, and stopped on the triangle by an off-ramp. The ever-reliable Dave showed up presently and the pair of them worked frantically to fix the puncture. They were in fear of their lives, with several near misses and two actual crashes, including a four car pile-up, occurring quite possibly because of the distraction they presented. A cop arrived and offered to help — as they do in America — but then went to help sort out the carnage further up the ramp. Roger and Gareth missed them after a few miles. Gareth performed a long, long circuit back through the freeway system looking for them, while Roger was posted along the motorway to stop them if they appeared. Soon enough the problem was fixed and we were all reunited.

We saw the sights of San Fran — the Golden Gate and Bay bridges by bike, then Alcatraz and the humps on Union Street down which the cars in the chase scene in the 1968 Steve McQueen film *Bullitt* get most of their airtime. We were amazed to find a large mature pohutukawa growing on the harbour foreshore — another member of the Kiwi diaspora.

From Frisco we headed east through some lovely country to the beautiful Yosemite National Park, where we camped for two nights, and then pushed on to Lone Pine at the perimeter of Death Valley. It was fiercely hot, easily as hot as anything we'd experienced in the deserts of Central Asia the year before. California was experiencing a heatwave at the time — 140 people had died by the time we immersed ourselves in it and the week before the temperature had reached 52 degrees Celsius. We'd hoped to experience Death Valley on its hottest day of the year so it looked as though the weather was conspiring to help us realise that ambition. Temperatures in the valley are routinely hotter by 20 degrees or so than they are further west.

We'd allowed two days for the crossing of the valley, which was tempting fate. It's only 217 km across, so taking two days meant we'd either have to waste time walking our bikes, get ourselves in some sort of trouble or organise sufficient side trips to use the time productively. In the event we managed all three.

We set out at 7 am, loaded down with water in case trouble

struck. As the sun mounted the sky the heat rose remarkably. We knew from our experiences in the Taklamakan Desert that you start doing strange things in elevated temperatures. That's Gareth's excuse, anyway — quite early in the first day he decided to ride off-piste into the sand and get a good photo of the bike amid the cacti. Unfortunately a 1200cc bike isn't quite as light as the 650cc machine he'd ridden in similar conditions on the Silk Road and it sank ungraciously not very far into this indulgence. This would have been fine had he not waved the other riders on, unwilling to keep them from whatever took their fancy down the road.

Dumb move.

Even with all the gear unloaded from the bike and with Gareth walking alongside it as he tried to drive it in gear back towards the road, he couldn't extricate it. The surface simply wasn't conducive. Every time he let the clutch out the wheel did paddlewheel imitations and the bike settled deeper. And once a heavy machine like that starts going over you're hard pressed to keep it upright. After several fruitless attempts, a bit of sweat and a lot of swearing, Gareth knew it was futile. He tried waving down the occasional passing motorist, which was equally futile. He resigned himself to the situation. There was to be no face-saving self-recovery.

Eventually (40 minutes, not the quickest of recoveries) the team returned and, sure enough, Gareth was forced to endure hoots, hollers and mandatory photos and movie takes before they even considered lending some muscle to extracting the bike.

More was to come. A couple of hours later at a roadhouse at Stovepipe Wells, Jo noticed Dave's bike had a flattish-looking back tyre. He ignored her advice to take advantage of the air-hose on site — not to mention the shade, cool drinks and air-conditioned roadhouse — and rode off into the shadeless expanse of desert. It must have been the heat. The air temperature was already 48 degrees and rising.

Sixteen kilometres down the road, about 80 m below sea-level, what should he hear but that old familiar blap-blap-blap of a flatty. Thank goodness for Jo's $6 compressor. Hand-pumping a mended tyre in this heat would have been no fun at all.

With our decision-making faculties clearly deficient in these temperatures, the call was made to retreat to the comfort of air-conditioned villas at Furnace Creek and leave the midday sun to mad dogs, Englishmen and ultra-marathon runners. We spent the afternoon sleeping off the morning's incompetence.

That evening, we rode to Zabriskie Point to enjoy the majestic sight of a Death Valley sunset. The temperature was still 50 degrees, having peaked at 52. You can only ride your bike in that heat if you're in full gear with vents closed to avoid getting scorched, and at a maximum of about 70 km/h. Otherwise the hot air behind your visor just burns your face up. As it was any bits of skin left exposed got burnt. But the sunset colours in the desert are unbeatable for photography and the location brought back memories of a 1970 hippie movie with the same name that was shot here. Its principal theme is rebellion against the United States forces of righteousness, eerily like the same forces that are afoot in America today.

Inspired though we were by our memories, we refrained from recreating the big dusty love-in that the movie features.

Next morning we were on the bikes by five in order to get out to Badwater, the lowest point in Death Valley, so named because all the water gravitates to this pan and, with nowhere else to go, evaporates, leaving behind a salt flat. The mercury had mercifully dropped to 38 degrees at this coolest time of the day so the temperature was comfortable.

We spent some time capturing the glory of the sunrise from a variety of vantage points, sharing them with a few real nutters who had just completed the annual Death Valley ultra-marathon and were now hobbling about capturing mementoes of the environment they had conquered. The fastest runner takes about 25 hours to complete the 217 km course, which runs from Badwater at 85 m below sea level to 2400 m up Mt Whitney, the tallest point in America's continental 49 states.

Compared with that our little adventure had been a doddle.

From Boulder City, Nevada, at the exit to Death Valley, we rode to Las Vegas to round our trip off with a night of hedonism and luxury. Then it was back to Los Angeles, where our bikes had a date with their crates.

It was all over, 29,000 km, nearly four months, three countries and 26 states of America later.

IN THE REAR-VIEW MIRROR

Another great trip! We're totally loving this idea of riding the world by bike. Every stage just leaves you hanging out for more.

We had thought North America would be a boring necessity — a stage of our traverse of the world that we'd just have to endure — being First World and coming with all the homogeneous blah that that entails: every town much like the last, every city just the same old template, everyone's values much the same as our own. Such was the stamp that CNN and Murdoch's definitions of 'news' and 'human interest' had placed on our impressions. We'd seen *Sex and the City* and *Desperate Housewives* — what more was there to the United States?

Totally wrong! Contrary to our expectations, America was a wonderful destination. It had a lot to do, we expect, with sticking to the backblocks, giving the cities a wide swerve and trying to touch those parts of America that don't much care for things beyond their county, let alone their state. The wonderful, self-imposed isolation is the key to understanding those 50 United States.

As for the riding, overall the roads may have been a little on the tame side but we managed to include enough gnarly interludes in our itinerary to make even the biking memorable. That Gareth, who has no patience for scenery, took away memories of the vast and diverse American landscape and became totally mesmerised by the wildlife was, to the rest of us, an achievement in itself — none so blind, after all, as those who will not see. Seems all that was needed was to scale the wildlife up to life-threatening proportions and he'd pay attention. That grizzly still stalks his nightmares. It was certainly an adrenaline-filled appetiser for Africa, the next stage on our circumnavigation.

We went from one extreme to another: from the most eastern part of the North American mainland to the most westerly; from the ferocious heat of the badlands of Mexico, Arizona, Utah and Nevada to the chill of the north and the freezing climes of the Beaufort and Bering seas; from the arid wasteland of White Sands to the teeming bayou of Louisiana; from the dire twang of country to the throb of rock'n'roll and the suave melodies of New Orleans jazz.

If there was a disappointment it was that we weren't able to spend as much time in the great outdoors as we'd intended. Gareth's commitments meant he was obliged to stay in touch with New Zealand for the bulk of the trip and that meant too many of our overnight stops saw us in civilisation. Bloody Gareth — why does he have to invite all four million of his closest Kiwi mates along for the ride? That said, as soon as Dave and Roger pitched in together and got their own computer, they became as addicted to communication as the rest of us and their media commitments burgeoned along the way.

Highlights? Well, let's summarise them for all who went. For Jo, as always, it was the people — not their psychology or anything fancy like that but, as with all the trips she's ever done, it's just being with them, making the connection, hearing their views on life, their joys and woes, that makes it all worthwhile. Dave is similar to Jo. For him too the people make the journey — and, of course, just to ride is the other buzz, anywhere, anytime. Roger had been really keen to get back to Alberta and the Yukon where he had family and to do all those roads he was familiar with, this time on two wheels. And for Gareth the highlights were the wildlife, the music and getting a better understanding of that good-ole-boy psyche.

So everyone had a purpose and everyone's highlights were many and varied. But for those of us whose offshore expedition rides have been pretty much all Third World, North America surprised by being far from the boring cruise we'd expected.

We found the American and Canadian people to be amazingly polite, helpful, warm and hospitable. It's not necessarily the image we have of North America from the outside, where our impressions tend to be formed by television shows and movies, usually set in the big cities and disproportionately featuring crime. The kindness of everyone we met, and even the simple friendliness and courtesy of people to one another in their daily lives, is at a level well above New Zealand, which prides itself on its hospitality and openness. After a matter of days in America, we found ourselves curbing our cussing and ready to smile and nod at strangers, just as the locals do.

There's always a deep sense of satisfaction when you complete a big expedition like this and everyone is in one piece, upright astride their still-functioning bikes and still talking to one another. We had very few problems, let alone serious ones. Apart from puncture repairs and the routine maintenance — oil and tyre changes, and chain lubes for Jo's — we hardly touched the bikes. They purred their way through everything we aimed them at.

As for the human element, we were again remarkably trouble-free. We all suffered not only from the Third World squirts in Mexico, but also from the First World squirts in California. We used to blame the lower food hygiene standards of the Third World but now rather suspect it's simply the strange combinations of food you ask your digestive system to cope with in the course of a trip. Eventually it reaches overload and just waves everything on through, much to our occasional discomfort.

Apart from Jo's alligator bite and the graze to Roger's hand in the Batopilas Canyon, the worst injury we suffered was Gareth's infected rear. His was a working schedule throughout the trip that was the equivalent of an adventure ride in and of itself: it was little wonder to the rest of us that his immune system suffered a blow-out under the stresses of his punishing schedule, in the form of a large boil that erupted painfully on his posterior. This necessitated a short stay at 'Doctor Jo's' hospital and a course of antibiotics but that was the extent of the incidence of ill-health our group suffered.

Just as hard as the technical challenges of handling a motorcycle, there's the group dynamics to cope with. We were all still mates at the end, even if there were moments on the way. Four people living in each other's faces for four months is bound to be something less than all beer and skittles — although the beer was bountiful. Everybody has down days and the others learn pretty quickly to give that person a wide berth as they wrestle with their demons. The biggest cause of upset is tiredness: riding day after day is great fun and each day brings new experiences but fatigue can tweak tempers to the boilover stage. Only Jo had the excuse of 'hormones' — the rest of us just got knackered. The occasional outburst when things aren't running smoothly is nature's way of telling others to steer clear. But it's amazing what healing powers necessity has, and the need to get back in the saddle and continue the journey always meant a disaffected camper would quickly recover and be back pulling their weight in the group pretty quickly.

Having others join the tour part-way through for short periods introduced a stress to the team dynamic we hadn't encountered on previous trips. By the time the new folk arrive, the group has already sorted out its routines and a new person can only disturb that. Each reacts in his or her own way: Gareth by mainly riding solo and figuring 'to hell with the corner-marking routine and trying to train up another monkey'; Dave by taking longer than normal to bring up the rear so everyone else has an enforced wait. There's no doubt that a team structure can be a fragile thing at times, though in the main the fact that the strength of the whole is greater than the sum of its individual resources is the factor that gets everyone through.

Against the above, it has to be acknowledged that the three of us — the pair of us and Dave — are a pretty tight unit these days, after years of expedition riding together and with the major Silk Road traverse behind us. It has got to be pretty tough for anyone to slot into the group. When you take this into account, the fact that everyone was still on speaking terms at journey's end seems little short of miraculous. Well done, Roger!

A s for America — we loved it, we learnt a lot more about it but it would be bold to say we now understand it. That, we suggest, is something that could only come from living your life there, and even then . . . It's the diversity of the place — human as well as geographic — that is forever defying visitors' attempts to comprehend it and generalise about it. The bayou people down south are just so different from the ranchers of Montana, who in turn have more in common with Canterbury hill farmers than they do with the folk of Nome, Alaska — or Alaskans generally, seeing how they all hibernate for a good part of the year. And as for the urbanites — well, we tried our darnedest to stay clear of those precincts so we can't really speak for them. Indeed, looking back, we made very few intrusions into Democrat territory — ours was definitely a redneck itinerary. And while we didn't make it to Muskogee, Oklahoma, we felt we met our fair share of Okies along the way. There's an innocence, if not a little intolerance of difference, about the Okies of America; the mental isolation that comes from living deep inside such a huge, diverse economic machine, produces both.

There are things to find fault with, of course — after all, this is the home of reality television, diseases of affluence, questionable invasions of other countries and ignorance on a major scale of life beyond America. And there's the religious fundamentalism, just about as scary as anything we saw in the Islamic countries along the Silk Road; the rabid patriotism, which we saw as no less virulent than Serbian nationalism; the deplorable, blind unsustainability of the ultra-materialistic American consume-or-die way of life; and the racism, of course. We could go on — but country music is just too easy to lampoon.

There's the noxious practice of tipping — don't get us started on that one. And, of course, there's American food. While we enjoyed some wonderful meals with Americans who invited us to dine with them, our tour of the greasy spoons of America didn't do a lot for us. By contrast, Mexican food and Canadian barbecues rock.

But these were niggles. As we've mentioned, you couldn't find more generous and friendly people, we loved the hands-off approach to regulation and the positive, service-oriented approach to law enforcement. We loved having the freedom to choose whether to wear our helmets, quite apart from everything else! We loved the free high-speed internet access available at hotels, motels and in wireless hotspots at airports, restaurants, even in parks here and there. We loved the price of petrol. And even country music got to us in the end — reminding us in no uncertain terms this was the US of A.

We were a little reluctant to go to America. But like Columbus we found so much more than we had expected. It was a true voyage of discovery. It was a blast.

What a trip. Roll on the next one!

ACKNOWLEDGEMENTS

Firstly to our riding buddies, Dave and Roger, a heartfelt thanks. You were great to be with, and it was a privilege to discover America in your company.

A number of people have helped on this project, most who don't feature in the text but without whom the book would remain just an idea.

Foremost of course is our writer John McCrystal, who has once more stepped in to actually get all the ideas and memories into a form suitable for publication. *Backblocks America* has been a very different project to *Silk Riders*, being less of a chronological tale of the route and the experiences along the way, but more of a thematic take on North American society, its politics and its values. We started the trip with a sketchy understanding but managed to fill it out substantially via the debates between ourselves and with the locals en route. It was John's suggestion that this was how the book should be shaped and we enjoyed the challenge he set.

Then there are the others in our World By Bike team who for one reason or another weren't along with us on this leg of our global traverse. They all provided support, good contacts in the States and handy hints as we undertook this four-month meander. MoD (Mike O'Donnell) and Brendan Keogh especially were great support from New Zealand.

As far as maintaining the website was concerned so that photos, blogs and the rest could be communicated readily to those back in New Zealand, Mike Bordignon and Dave Bruce once again kept the technology fires burning. Thanks guys.

To our commercial partners at BMW, Icebreaker and John Baker Insurance, once again a big thanks: we hope you were satisfied with any coverage you got. We'd be using your products anyway so we're grateful that you can see value in what we're doing.

To our various hosts along the way, including Bob Chappell on Eleuthera Island in the Bahamas; his daughter Anne and friends Mark and Bodile from Sebastopol, California; Ernie and Susan Conover up in Ohio; Howard and Judy Evans of Billings, Montana; Gordy and Judy Westberg of Whitehorse; Matt, Loretta and Aiden Anderson in Fairbanks; Steve, Christine and Stephanie Elder in Vancouver; John MacLean and Leyette and Paul Callister in Seattle — and I'm sure others we can't recall — thanks so much for the hospitality and friendship you extended. We will not forget it.

To the folks at Random House — Jenny, Nic, Sarah and all the others there who had to put up with our erratic behaviour through the preparation of this manuscript. Your stability is admired!

Finally, thanks to those of our families who stay behind and allow us this indulgence to skip around the globe. We know we're very lucky being the recipients of such tolerance and are doing our best to enjoy that.

And so to Africa.

Gareth and Jo Morgan

Gareth Morgan

Economist, portfolio investor, motorcycle adventurer and chronically addicted fisherman — Gareth has never really fitted well with the mainstream but his larger-than-life persona has won him many fans and more than a few foes. If nothing else, applying the blowtorch of economic theory to expose sector interests acting against national wellbeing tends to cause reaction.

For all that, he has instigated two successful and well-known New Zealand businesses: the economics consultancy Infometrics, and Gareth Morgan Investments (www. garethmorgan.com), his personal portfolio management business.

Joanne (Jo) Morgan

Arguably the saner of the pair, Jo's adult life has spanned a spectrum of interests — from welding to social work, importing (when New Zealand was trade-protected and profit margins were to die for), bus driving, teaching, studying languages, and mechanical repairs. Oh, and besides all that she brought up four children and ran a home as Gareth travelled New Zealand spreading the economic word.

Jo tried to expose her young children early to the realities of others' lives: in Smokey Mountain, Manila; on the Afghanistan–Pakistan border in the Hindu Kush; and in Korean primary schools. She hoped this would also foster in them a love of travel and appreciation of other cultures.

These days, in a space few females are prepared to enter, Jo's motorcycling exploits have seen her handstanding on her bike while crossing the salt pans of Bolivia, trading in the floating flower market on Dal Lake in Kashmir, rock-hopping an Enfield up the Himalayan slopes of Nepal, and plummeting down the world's most dangerous road in Bolivia.

Her enthusiasm for the extraordinary has not dampened her commitment to her home, and Jo continues to play an active role in the politics and life of her community.

Now with a grown-up family, Gareth and Jo — when not doting on their two granddaughters — have widened their activities to roaming the globe, which enables Gareth to experience first-hand the businesses, societies and economies his portfolios are invested in.

The details of their global traverse by motorcycle are recorded on www.worldbybike.com